W9-CFF-199

HARCOURT SCHOOL PUBLISHERS

STORYtown

ENGLISH-LANGUAGE LEARNERS

STUDENT HANDBOOK

Harcourt
SCHOOL PUBLISHERS
www.harcourtschool.com

Copyright © by Harcourt, Inc.

All rights reserved. No part of this publication may be reproduced or transmitted in any form or by any means, electronic or mechanical, including photocopy, recording, or any information storage and retrieval system, without permission in writing from the publisher.

Requests for permission to make copies of any part of the work should be addressed to School Permissions and Copyrights, Harcourt, Inc., 6277 Sea Harbor Drive, Orlando, Florida 32887-6777. Fax: 407-345-2418.

STORYTOWN is a trademark of Harcourt, Inc. HARCOURT and the Harcourt Logo are trademarks of Harcourt, Inc., registered in the United States of America and/or other jurisdictions.

Printed in the United States of America

ISBN 10 0-15-367056-8

ISBN 13 978-0-15-367056-5

If you have received these materials as examination copies free of charge, Harcourt School Publishers retains title to the materials and they may not be resold. Resale of examination copies is strictly prohibited and is illegal.

Possession of this publication in print format does not entitle users to convert this publication, or any portion of it, into electronic format.

1 2 3 4 5 6 7 8 9 10 197 16 15 14 13 12 11 10 09 08 07

C O N T E N T S

CONTENTS

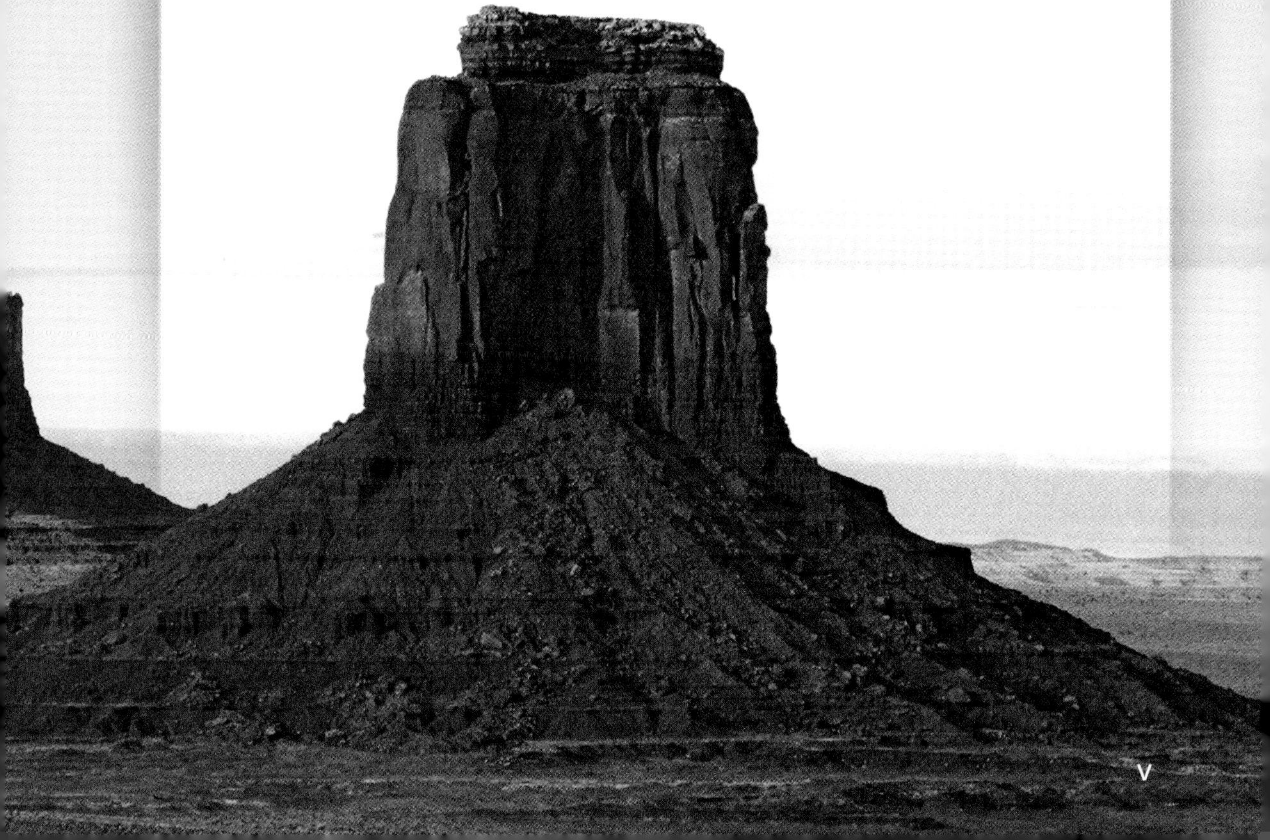

Use What You Know

You can use what you know to help you understand what you read.

The puma is a large member of the cat family. Pumas are wild animals. They live by hunting other animals. A puma can grow to be five feet long, not counting the tail. Long ago, pumas lived throughout the forests of the United States. Today, though, they live only in places where few people live.

- **Use prior knowledge**
  "I know what a cat is like. A puma probably looks like a big cat."

- **Reason**
  "I know that wild animals live in wild places. When people built towns in wild places, many pumas must have lost their homes."

- **Think about expressions**
  "I think *not counting* means *not including*. A puma can be five feet long, not including the tail."

Find Help

If you need help understanding what you read, look around you.

The manatee is a large mammal that lives in the water. Manatees eat water plants. One manatee can eat up to 100 pounds of plants in a day. The manatee's body is just right for water. Its front legs are shaped like paddles. It has no hind legs at all.

- **Use a computer**

  "What does a manatee look like? Maybe I can find a picture of this animal on the Internet."

- **Use books**

  "The dictionary says that hind legs are back legs. It also tells me that *hind* had the long sound of *i*."

- **Ask for help**

  "I can ask my teacher, a friend, or a family member how to say *manatee*."

Make Connections

Try to make connections between what you read
and your own experience.

Anika pulled the hood of her parka tighter around her face. A freezing November wind howled across the ice. There was nothing but white as far as Anika could see. She was still two miles from camp. The Alaska days were short at this time of year. With luck, Anika would get to camp before dark.

- **Reuse language**

  "I think *with luck* must be a way to say *if she is lucky*."

- **Use context**

  "*Howled* tells what the wind was doing. It must have been blowing strongly."

- **Compare and contrast**

  "I can compare Alaska with my home. They are not alike at all! Alaska is colder and has more snow."

Picture It

Making pictures in your mind can help you understand.

When I first got my puppy, he was like a little ball of fur. He was fluffy and soft with bright brown eyes. He is not a puppy anymore. Now he is huge! His head comes up to my chin.

- **Make pictures in your head**
  as a puppy . . .
  now . . .

- **Describe it**
  "I can tell someone else about a subject
  to help me picture it and remember it."

- **Memorize**
  "I can look for important
  words that describe the
  subject. Then I can read
  them over and over until
  I remember them."

Look for Patterns

Looking for words and word parts that are the same
can help you understand what you read.

The ants go marching one by one.
It's fun, it's fun.
The ants go marching one by one.
It's fun, it's fun.
The ants go marching one by one.
They tell the littlest not to run.
The ants go marching two by two.
It's true, it's true.
The ants go marching two by two.

_____.

The ants go marching two by two.
The littlest stops to tie its shoe.

- **Think about word families**
  "*Littlest* looks like *little,* which means the same as *small.* I think littlest means the same as *smallest.*"

- **Use repetition**
  "*It's fun, it's fun* repeats in the first verse. I think *It's true, it's true* will repeat in the second verse."

- **Use rhyme**
  "I'm not sure how to say *shoe,* but I know that it rhymes with *two.* It must have the /o͞o/ vowel sound."

x

Set a Purpose

Think about what you want to learn or tell.

When Wilma Rudolph was a young girl, she wore a leg brace to help her walk. She also worked hard to walk without the brace. She did exercises to strengthen her leg, and she did walk without the brace.

At age 12, Wilma decided to become an athlete. She trained hard to be the best runner she could be. Her hard work paid off. In 1960, she became the first American woman to win three gold medals in the Olympics.

- **Set a purpose for listening**
  "I will listen to learn facts about Wilma Rudolph's life."

- **Set a purpose for speaking**
  "I want to persuade younger students to join the track team."

- **Set a purpose for reading**
  "I want to find out how Wilma became such a good runner."

- **Set a purpose for writing**
  "I want to write about famous women athletes."

Background and Vocabulary

Selections You Will Read
- "The Hot and Cold Summer"
- "Secret Talk"

"The Hot and Cold Summer" is **realistic fiction.**
Realistic fiction has characters and events that are
like people and events in real life. As you read, look for:
- a setting that is familiar to most readers
- realistic characters and events

What is "The Hot and Cold Summer" about?

This selection is about how three friends spend their
summer. Two friends sell lemonade at a lemonade stand.
One friend goes away to a summer camp.

▲ Lemonade stand

▲ Swimming pool at a
summer camp

What vocabulary will you learn?

Robust Vocabulary

pact

queasy

foisted

venture

annoyed

depriving

Tip

As you learn new words, remember to write them in your Vocabulary Log. Which words do you know very well? Which words are you still learning?

Word Bank

lounge chair

bike

slice

whole pie

vegetables

celery

carrot

puzzle

3

Comprehension

What is the focus skill in this lesson?

The focus skill is **Character's Traits and Motivations.**
A character's traits show what he or she is like. A character's
motivations are the reasons he or she acts in a certain way.
The actions of the characters in a story are related to their traits
and motivations.

Read the passage.

> My friend Mara broke her leg one week before summer vacation
> started! I felt very bad for her. I wondered how I could make her
> summer fun. This is what I decided to do: every week, I would go
> someplace new with Mara. I wanted to make sure that Mara's
> summer was great!

Traits: The person telling the story is kind. She is a good friend.

Motivation: She wants Mara to have fun during the summer,
even though she has a broken leg.

This girl is helping her friend. ▶

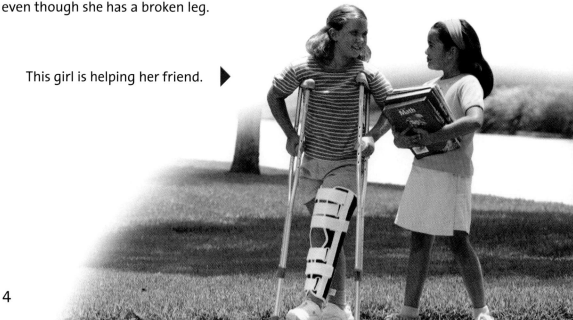

4

Grammar and Writing

What kind of writing will you do in the lesson?

You will write a **character description.** A character description tells what a character is like. It includes details about what the character says and does. Here is the beginning of a character description:

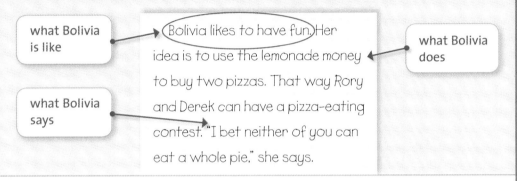

what Bolivia is like

what Bolivia does

what Bolivia says

Bolivia likes to have fun. Her idea is to use the lemonade money to buy two pizzas. That way Rory and Derek can have a pizza-eating contest. "I bet neither of you can eat a whole pie," she says.

What is the grammar skill?

You will learn about **declarative sentences** and **interrogative sentences.**

Rory sits in a lounge chair.

Did Derek come home from camp?

declarative sentence

interrogative sentence

Decoding-Spelling Connection

Most words with the consonant-vowel-consonant pattern have a short vowel sound in that part.

short vowel sound

brick   **br**   **i**   **ck**

consonant-vowel-consonant pattern

Background and Vocabulary

Selections You Will Read
- "Mighty Jackie: The Strike-Out Queen"
- "The New Kid"

"Mighty Jackie: The Strike-Out Queen" is a **biography.** A biography tells about a person's life. It is written by another person. As you read, look for:
- opinions and personal judgments based on facts
- information about why the person is important

What is "Mighty Jackie: The Strike-Out Queen" about?

This selection is about real baseball players of the 1930s. You will read about a girl who pitched against a famous men's baseball team. Why do you think the girl did this? What did she want to prove?

▼ A baseball game

batter

pitcher

umpire

home plate

6

What vocabulary will you learn?

Robust Vocabulary

legendary

gaped

snickering

stunned

muttered

flinched

glared

fluke

Tip

Be a Word Detective! Look for these words in newspapers, magazines, and books. Listen for the words on the radio or television.

glove and ball

Word Bank

bleachers

ball field

diamond

base

Comprehension

What is the focus skill in this lesson?

The focus skill is **Character's Traits and Motivations.**
Remember that a character's **traits** are what the character is
like. A character's **motivations** are the reasons the character
acts in a certain way. The story **setting** is when and where it
happens. The setting may play a role in what a character does.

Read the passage.

Raul stood on the pitcher's
mound. He had practiced hard all
week. He had pitched to his brother
every day. Raul wanted to make his
brother proud. He threw the first
pitch of the game. It was a strike!

Traits: Raul is hard-working and
determined.

Motivation: Raul wants his brother
to be proud of him.

Grammar and Writing

What kind of writing will you do in the lesson?

You will write a **description of a place.** You will describe what you can see, hear, and smell there. Here is a description of a ballpark:

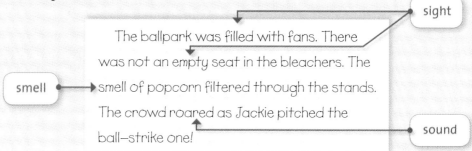

The ballpark was filled with fans. There was not an empty seat in the bleachers. The smell of popcorn filtered through the stands. The crowd roared as Jackie pitched the ball—strike one!

sight

smell

sound

What is the grammar skill?

You will learn about **imperative sentences** and **exclamatory sentences.**

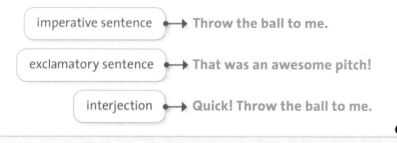

imperative sentence → **Throw the ball to me.**

exclamatory sentence → **That was an awesome pitch!**

interjection → **Quick! Throw the ball to me.**

Decoding–Spelling Connection

Some words break into syllables after the vowel or vowels. These syllables usually have a long vowel sound.

season

| sea | son |

Baseball season has 162 games. ▶

Background and Vocabulary

Selections You Will Read

• "Danitra Brown Leaves Town"
• "Summertime Star Parties"

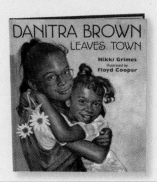

"Danitra Brown Leaves Town" is narrative poetry. A narrative poem is a poem that tells a story. As you read, look for:

• characters, a setting, and plot events
• rhythm and rhyming words

What is "Danitra Brown Leaves Town" about?

This selection is about two friends who live in a city. The two friends say goodbye for the summer. One friend goes to the country. The other friend stays in the city. What things do you see in a city? What things do you see in the country?

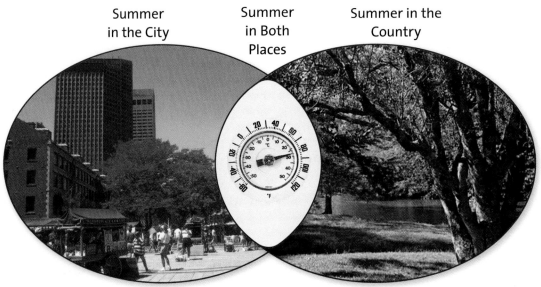

Summer in the City

Summer in Both Places

Summer in the Country

What vocabulary will you learn?

Robust Vocabulary

surrender

particular

sparkling

clusters

sizzles

stroll

Tip

Remember to look in the Glossary for explanations of the words. What other strategies can you use?

Word Bank

fireworks

barbecue

boardwalk

picnic

reunion

Comprehension

What is the focus skill in this lesson?

The focus skill is **Compare and Contrast.** Authors sometimes
compare and contrast people, places, or things in a story.
When you compare, you tell how two people, places, or things
are alike. When you contrast, you tell how two people, places,
or things are different.

Read the passage.

Monica and Alexa are best friends. They both like to read. Monica
likes books about horses. Alexa likes scary books. During the summer,
Monica and Alexa like to read together under a shady tree.

Alike: Monica and Alexa are both girls. They both like to read.
Different: Monica likes books about horses, while Alexa likes scary books.

Grammar and Writing

What kind of writing will you do in the lesson?

You will write a **narrative poem**—a poem that tells a story.
The poem may have a **rhythm.** Some words may **rhyme.**
Here is part of a narrative poem:

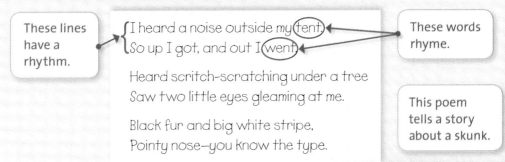

These lines have a rhythm.

I heard a noise outside my tent,
So up I got, and out I went.

These words rhyme.

Heard scritch-scratching under a tree
Saw two little eyes gleaming at me.

Black fur and big white stripe,
Pointy nose—you know the type.

This poem tells a story about a skunk.

What is the grammar skill?

You will learn about the two parts of a sentence: the **subject** and the **predicate.**

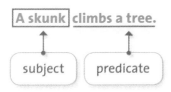

A skunk | climbs a tree.

subject   predicate

Decoding–Spelling Connection

Different pairs of letters can stand for the same vowel sound.

| au̲ction | ble̲w | cho̲i̲ce |
| aw̲ful | spo̲o̲n | anno̲y̲ed |

Background and Vocabulary

Selections You Will Read

- "Kai's Journey to Gold Mountain"
- "My Japanese Sister"

"Kai's Journey to Gold Mountain" is **historical fiction.**
Historical fiction is set in the past and portrays people,
places, and events that did happen or could have
happened. As you read, look for:

- a setting that is a real time and place in the past
- realistic characters and events

What is "Kai's Journey to Gold Mountain" about?

This story is about a boy who was born in China in the
1930s. He traveled by ship to the United States to be with
his father. The boy spent many weeks on an island in
San Francisco Bay, waiting to find out if he would be
allowed to enter the United States.

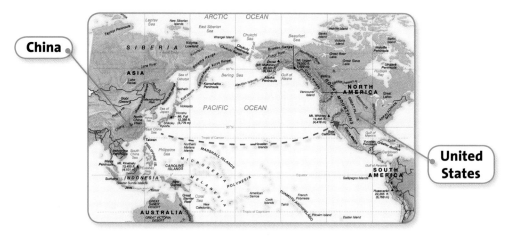

▲ Ship route from China to the United States

What vocabulary will you learn?

Robust Vocabulary

averted

fury

interrogation

stern

accusing

solemnly

cringed

craned

Tip
Thinking about the other words in a sentence can help you figure out a new word. What other strategies can you use?

Word Bank

porridge

bunk

script

letter

guard

15

Comprehension

What is the focus skill in this lesson?

The focus skill is **Compare and Contrast.** Remember that when you compare, you tell how two or more things are alike. When you contrast, you tell how two or more things are different.

Read the passage.

> Ellis Island and Angel Island are both islands. Ellis Island is on the east coast, near New York City. Angel Island is on the west coast, near San Francisco. During the 1800s and early 1900s, the islands were the first stop for many immigrants who came to the United States.

Alike: Both Angel Island and Ellis Island are islands near a coast. Both islands were immigration stations.

Different: Ellis Island is on the east coast, but Angel Island is on the west coast.

▼ Angel Island immigration station

Grammar and Writing

What kind of writing will you do in the lesson?

You will write a **journal entry.** A journal entry tells about your own experiences. This is an example of a journal entry:

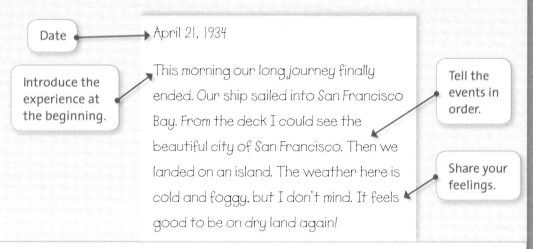

Date → April 21, 1934

Introduce the experience at the beginning. → This morning our long journey finally ended. Our ship sailed into San Francisco Bay. From the deck I could see the beautiful city of San Francisco. Then we landed on an island. The weather here is cold and foggy, but I don't mind. It feels good to be on dry land again!

Tell the events in order.

Share your feelings.

What is the grammar skill?

You will learn about **complete and simple subjects and predicates.**

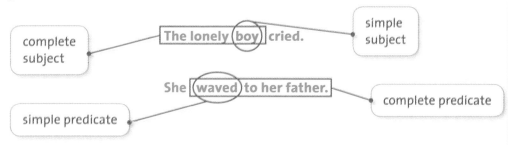

complete subject — The lonely (boy) cried. — simple subject

She (waved) to her father. — complete predicate

simple predicate

Decoding–Spelling Connection

You will learn about words that have the endings -*ed* and -*ing*.

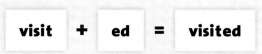

visit + ed = visited

17

Background and Vocabulary

READERS' THEATER

COMPREHENSION STRATEGIES

Selections You Will Read

You will read a selection titled "Pedro Puts On a Play." The selection is a **Readers' Theater.**

You will also read a story titled "Raul's After–School Snack." This selection is **realistic fiction.** Realistic fiction contains characters and events that could exist in real life.

What are the selections about?

"Pedro Puts On a Play" is about a boy who puts on a puppet show for his class.

"Raul's After–School Snack" is about a boy who thinks he is eating cookies. He is surprised when he finds out what the snack really is.

puppets

a snack

18

What vocabulary will you learn?

Robust Vocabulary

culinary

downcast

consternation

vivid

extensive

serenely

reminiscent

pensive

recruit

commenced

Tip

Thinking about the other words in a sentence can help you figure out the meaning of a word. What other strategies can you use?

dog biscuits

Word Bank

mariachi

cookies

recipe

How to Make Lemonade

First, have a grown-up squeeze the juice from several lemons.

1. Mix the lemon juice with water.
2. Add sugar until the lemonade is sweet enough.

"Bow wow!"

Fluency

As you read "Pedro Puts On a Play," you will review the two fluency skills you practiced in Theme 1. When you read a script aloud, remember to:

• read with **accuracy**

• use appropriate **reading rate** to help you and your listeners understand your lines

Comprehension Strategies

As you read "Raul's After-School Snack," you will review the two comprehension strategies you learned in Theme 1.

• **Use Story Structure**   Use story structure to help you understand the characters, setting, and plot.

• **Answer Questions**   When you come across a question about something that happens in a story, you can use what you know from life to help you answer the question.

Writing

In Theme 1, you wrote several compositions. In Lesson 5, you will choose one of these compositions to revise. Choose a composition that you would like to add to your Writing Portfolio.

> **Tip**
>
> **Writing Traits** When you revise your writing, try to let your own personal **voice** come through.
>
> Look at your **choice of words** and make sure that:
> • you have chosen colorful words
> • you have used the exact words you need

SAMPLE REVISION

Look at how the first paragraph below was revised. What makes the revised paragraph better?

> I have two talents. cooking and art. One day I decided to use the talents to make one good thing. I wanted to make a building out of bread.

> I have two talents: baking and making sculptures. One day I decided to use both of my talents to make one spectacular creation. I planned to construct a house out of delicious homemade gingerbread!

Background and Vocabulary

Selections You Will Read
- "On the Banks of Plum Creek"
- "Surviving on the Prairie"

"On the Banks of Plum Creek" is **historical fiction.**
Historical fiction is based on a real time and place in
the past. The events, characters, and other details may
be imagined. As you read, look for:
- realistic characters and events
- a setting that is a real time and place in the past

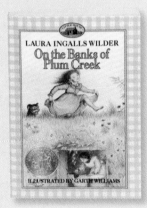

What is "On the Banks of Plum Creek" about?

This selection is about the Ingalls family. They were settlers
who lived in Minnesota during the 1870s. The main characters
are Laura Ingalls and her older sister, Mary. The girls take care
of their family's home while their parents and baby sister
are away.

Minnesota

▼ Settlers farm the land.

What vocabulary will you learn?

Robust Vocabulary

responsible

darted

jostling

swerved

attentive

pounced

contradicting

Tip
Remember to look in the Glossary for explanations of the words. What other strategies can you use?

Word Bank

oxen and covered wagon

cattle

creek

prairie

hay-stacks

Comprehension

What is the focus skill in this lesson?

The focus skill is **Plot: Conflict and Resolution.** All stories have a **plot,** or a series of events. Every plot has a **conflict** and its **resolution.** The conflict is the problem or challenge faced by the main characters. It usually is introduced early in the story. The resolution is the solution to the conflict. It usually happens near the end of a story.

Read the passage.

> David and John were arguing. Pa was going to town for the day, and both boys wanted to go. However, one of them had to stay home to take care of the farm. Pa thought of a number between one and ten. The boys each guessed a number. David picked the exact number, so he went to town with Pa.

- **Conflict:** Both David and John wanted to go to town, but one boy had to stay home.
- **Resolution:** Pa told the boys to pick a number between one and ten, and David picked the right number.

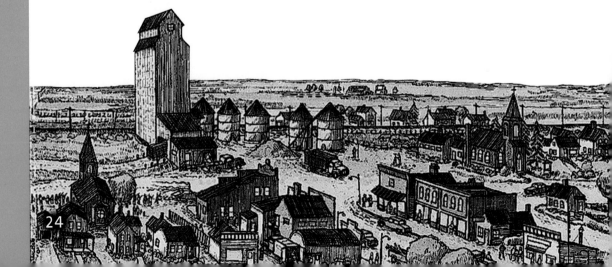

Grammar and Writing

What kind of writing will you do in the lesson?

You will write a **summary**. A summary tells the most important information in a story. Look at the story and summary below.

> A summary tells the most important events.

> A summary is short.

Story: The cattle stood at the hay-stacks, eating the hay. Mary and Laura watched in shock. Then Laura grabbed a big stick. She ran toward the cattle, waving the stick at them. She shouted to her sister to help her scare the cows away. Mary felt scared, but she hurried after Laura.

Story Summary: Mary and Laura saw the cattle eating the hay-stacks. The sisters ran toward the cows, trying to scare them away.

What is the grammar skill?

You will learn about **compound subjects** and **compound predicates**.

compound subject

Juan plays in the creek.
Mei plays in the creek. → Juan and Mei play in the creek.

compound predicate

Jarrell sings.
Jarrell plays guitar. → Jarrell sings and plays guitar.

Decoding–Spelling Connection

Words ending with consonant + -le are divided into syllables before the consonant in the last syllable.

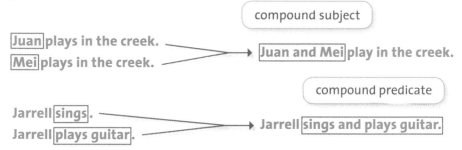

fable   candle

| fa | ble | can | dle |

Lesson 7

Background and Vocabulary

Selections You Will Read
- "Justin and the Best Biscuits in the World"
- "Home on the Range," "Hats off to the Cowboy"

"Justin and the Best Biscuits in the World" is **realistic fiction.** Realistic fiction has characters and events that are like people and events in real life. As you read, look for:
- realistic characters and events
- challenges and problems that might happen in real life

What is "Justin and the Best Biscuits in the World" about?

This selection is about Justin, a boy who lives in the city. Justin visits his grandfather on a ranch. At the ranch, Justin helps his grandfather do chores. While doing the work, Justin learns many new skills.

In a city, chores might include jobs in and around the house. ▶

Chores
Make bed ☐
Feed cat ☐
Set table ☑
Empty trash ☐
Fold clothes ☐

▼ On a ranch, chores include both household tasks and other jobs.

What vocabulary will you learn?

Robust Vocabulary

reluctant

rumpled

surge

inspecting

taut

untangled

resounded

lurked

Tip

As you learn new words, remember to write them in your Vocablulary Log. Which words do you know very well? Which words are you still learning?

Word Bank

barbed wire fence

rodeo

pancakes

biscuits

doe and fawn

27

Comprehension

What is the focus skill in this lesson?

The focus skill is **Plot: Conflict and Resolution.**
Remember that the plot of every story contains a **conflict,** or
problem, that the characters must solve. The **resolution** of the
plot shows how the conflict is solved.

Read the passage.

> The hungry cowboys stopped for lunch. Grandpa built a small fire.
> He took cooking things and some food out of his pack. Then he asked
> Mario to cook the food. Mario didn't know how to cook over a fire!
> He didn't know what to do. Another cowboy saw Mario's frightened
> look. "I'll help you," the cowboy said.

- **Conflict:** Mario must cook lunch over a fire, but he doesn't know how.
- **Resolution:** A cowboy offers to help.

Grammar and Writing

What kind of writing will you do in the lesson?

You will write a **narrative.** A narrative tells a story that has a beginning, middle, and end. Here is the beginning of a narrative:

The sky was still dark when the cowboys got out of bed. They ate a big breakfast of biscuits and bacon. As the morning sun rose, they went to the barn and saddled their horses. They were ready for a long day of herding cattle.

What is the grammar skill?

You will learn about **simple sentences** and **compound sentences.**

two simple sentences: Grandpa cooks dinner. Justin washes the dishes.

comma and connecting conjunction

one compound sentence: Grandpa cooks dinner **, and** Justin washes the dishes.

Decoding–Spelling Connection

Words with a double-consonant pattern are usually divided into syllables between the pair of consonants.

supper   **rabbit**

| sup | per | | rab | bit |

29

Background and Vocabulary

Selections You Will Read

- "Three Little Cyberpigs"
- "The Three Little Pigs Revisited"

"Three Little Cyberpigs" is a **play.** Plays are stories that are performed for an audience. As you read, look for:

- characters' names introducing dialogue
- stage directions describing how the characters move on stage

What is "Three Little Cyberpigs" about?

This selection is about three pigs who visit a computer store. The pigs meet many different characters. The pigs learn how to use computers.

What vocabulary will you learn?

Robust Vocabulary

slick

nimble

impressed

cease

exist

fierce

Tip

Be a Word Detective! Look for these words in newspapers, magazines and books. Listen for the words on the radio or television.

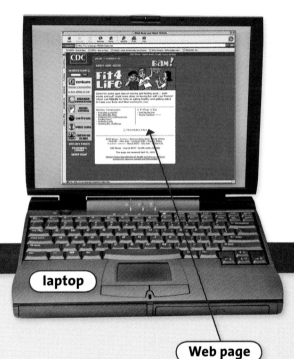

Word Bank

file

Ann, tour guide to cyberspace

laptop

Web page

customer

31

Comprehension

What is the focus skill in this lesson?

The focus skill is **Author's Purpose and Perspective.**
The **author's purpose** is the reason why the author writes a
selection. It may be to entertain, to inform, to persuade, or to
teach a lesson. The **author's perspective** is the author's point
of view about the topic of the selection.

Read the passage.

> Mother Goose is not a goose or a person. She is not real at all.
> She is the imaginary author of many children's rhymes. Mother Goose
> gave us rhymes about Humpty Dumpty and Little Miss Muffett. She
> told us about Jack and Jill and Little Bo Beep. Her nursery rhymes are
> a lot of fun!

Author's purpose: to tell readers who Mother Goose was

Author's perspective: Mother Goose's stories are fun to read.

Little Miss Muffett ▶

◀ Little Bo Beep

Grammar and Writing

What kind of writing will you do in this lesson?

You will write an **e-mail.** You will organize your writing with a beginning, a middle, and an ending. Here is an example of an e-mail:

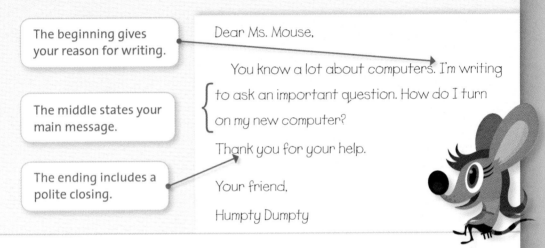

The beginning gives your reason for writing.

The middle states your main message.

The ending includes a polite closing.

Dear Ms. Mouse,

You know a lot about computers. I'm writing to ask an important question. How do I turn on my new computer?

Thank you for your help.

Your friend,

Humpty Dumpty

What is the grammar skill?

You will learn about **prepositional phrases.**

preposition

prepositional phrase

Jack sits (at) the computer.

object of the preposition

Decoding–Spelling Connection

Syllables with two consonants in the middle can be divided in different ways.

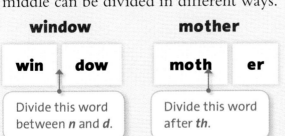

window

| win | dow |

Divide this word between *n* and *d*.

mother

| moth | er |

Divide this word after *th*.

Background and Vocabulary

Selections You Will Read

- "Weaving A California Tradition"
- "Wonder Weaver"

"Weaving A California Tradition" is **expository nonfiction.**
Expository nonfiction gives you information about a topic.
As you read, look for:

- facts and details about a topic
- photographs and captions
- graphics such as maps, diagrams, or charts

What is "Weaving a California Tradition" about?

This selection is about a Native American family who makes traditional crafts. The family gathers materials from plants, prepares the materials, and then uses the materials to weave beautiful baskets.

▼ Weaving a basket

▼ Gathering plant materials

What vocabulary will you learn?

Robust Vocabulary

unique

infest

intervals

delicate

flexible

bond

inspires

preserve

Tip

Remember to look in the Glossary for explanations of the words. What other strategies can you use?

Word Bank

tightly woven

bundle

coils

loosely woven

exhibit of baskets

design

Comprehension

What is the focus skill in this lesson?

The focus skill is **Author's Purpose and Perspective.**
Remember that every author has a **purpose** for writing. An
author may write to entertain, to inform, to persuade, or to
teach. An author may have a **perspective,** or feelings about the
subject of his or her writing.

Read the passage.

American Indians have been making pottery for thousands of years.
Today Southwestern Indian pottery is especially famous. Many of
the pots have interesting shapes, such as the wedding vase with two
spouts. The beautiful pots are also famous for their colorful designs
and figures.

Author's purpose: to give facts about Southwestern Indian pottery

Author's perspective: Southwestern Indian pottery is beautiful and
interesting.

▼ Pottery

Grammar and Writing

What kind of writing will you do in this lesson?

You will write an **explanatory paragraph.** An explanatory paragraph explains something. Here is a short explanatory paragraph:

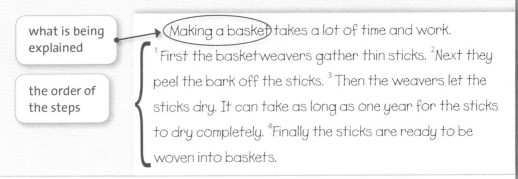

what is being explained

the order of the steps

Making a basket takes a lot of time and work. [1] First the basketweavers gather thin sticks. [2] Next they peel the bark off the sticks. [3] Then the weavers let the sticks dry. It can take as long as one year for the sticks to dry completely. [4] Finally the sticks are ready to be woven into baskets.

What is the grammar skill?

You will learn about **complex sentences.**

dependent clause

independent clause

Complex sentence: When weavers collect plants, they choose them carefully.

Decoding–Spelling Connection

When dividing words with three consonants in the middle, keep together the consonants that are blends. Also keep together the consonants that stand for one sound.

merchant

| mer | chant |

ch = one sound

pumpkin

| pump | kin |

mp = blend

Background and Vocabulary

Selections You Will Read

You will read a selection titled "Emerald's Eggs." The selection is a **Readers' Theater.**

You will also read a selection titled "Local Governments." This **social studies** selection gives facts about city government.

READERS' THEATER

COMPREHENSION STRATEGIES

What are the selections about?

"Emerald's Eggs" is about some fourth graders who help protect turtle eggs on a Texas beach.

"Local Governments" explains how local governments are organized and what they do for the community.

sea turtle

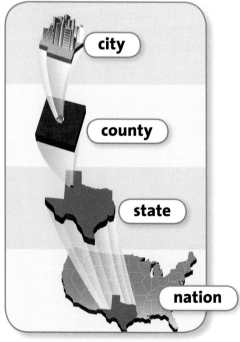

city

county

state

nation

What vocabulary will you learn?

Robust Vocabulary

comprehend

pliable

solitary

scan

vulnerable

exuberant

mature

lumbers

encircle

nurture

Tip

Remember to look in the Glossary for explanations of the words. What other strategies can you use?

eggs

nest

Word Bank

sand dune

binoculars

emerald

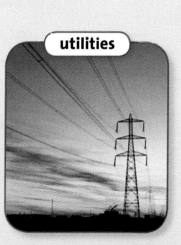

utilities

Fluency

As you read "Emerald's Eggs," you will review the two fluency skills you practiced in Theme 2. When you read a script aloud, remember to:

- change your **intonation** to show the feelings of each character
- use **phrasing** to pause between groups of words

Comprehension Strategies

As you read "Local Governments," you will review the two comprehension strategies you learned in Theme 2.

- **Monitor Comprehension: Reread**   If you have questions about what you are reading, try rereading. Maybe you missed some important information.
- **Summarize**   As you read, pause to sum up the most important ideas.

local government

▼ An elected official speaks with local residents.

40

Writing

In Theme 2, you wrote several compositions. In Lesson 10, you will choose one of these compositions to revise. Choose a composition that you would like to add to your Writing Portfolio.

> **Tip**
>
> **Writing Traits** When you revise your writing, make sure that all your **ideas** are focused on the topic.
>
> Make sure that your ideas are **organized** in a way that makes sense.

SAMPLE REVISION

Look at how the first paragraph below was revised. What makes the revised paragraph better?

> Sea turtles come ashore to lay their eggs. She lays her eggs inside the hole. First the mother turtle digs a hole in the sand. Many animals dig holes. Then she covers the eggs with sand.

> Sea turtles come ashore to lay their eggs. First the mother turtle digs a hole in the sand. She lays her eggs inside the hole. Then she covers the eggs with sand.

Background and Vocabulary

Selections You Will Read
- "Mimicry and Camouflage"
- "lizards, frogs, and polliwogs"

"Mimicry and Camouflage" is **expository nonfiction.** Expository nonfiction gives facts and information about a topic. As you read, look for:
- photographs and captions
- text structure—the way ideas are organized

What is "Mimicry and Camouflage" about?

This selection is about how living things use mimicry and camouflage to survive.

Mimicry means looking like or acting like something else. When you mimic something, you copy it.

Camouflage means looking like what is around you. It is hard to see an animal that is using camouflage.

mimicry

camouflage

What vocabulary will you learn?

Robust Vocabulary

predators

traits

lure

mimic

resembles

obvious

deceptive

avoid

Tip

Remember to look in the Glossary for explanations of the words. What other strategies can you use?

tiger

Word Bank

grasshopper

butterfly

forest

desert

43

Comprehension

What is the focus skill in this lesson?

The focus skill is **Text Structure: Cause and Effect.**
Nonfiction sometimes tells about causes and effects. A cause
makes something else happen. An effect is what happens. When
a selection uses many causes and effects, we say that it has a text
structure of cause and effect.

Read the passage.

> Snowshoe hares have brown fur for most of the
> year. However, in places where it snows, their fur
> changes color! The coming of winter causes the
> hare's coat to change to snowy white. This allows
> the snowshoe hare to blend with its surroundings.

- The coming of winter is the cause.
- The hare's fur changing to white is the effect.

A snowshoe hare in winter ▶

44

Grammar and Writing

What kind of writing will you do in this lesson?

You will write a **cause-and-effect composition.** You will organize your writing with causes and effects. Here is a short cause-and-effect composition:

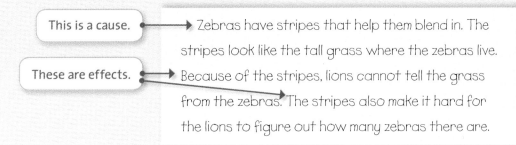

This is a cause. → Zebras have stripes that help them blend in. The stripes look like the tall grass where the zebras live.

These are effects. → Because of the stripes, lions cannot tell the grass from the zebras. The stripes also make it hard for the lions to figure out how many zebras there are.

What is the grammar skill?

You will learn about **common nouns** and **proper nouns.**

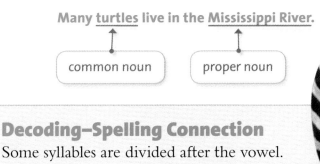

Many <u>turtles</u> live in the <u>Mississippi River</u>.

common noun   proper noun

Decoding–Spelling Connection

Some syllables are divided after the vowel.
Some syllables are divided after the consonant.

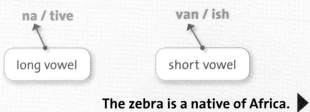

na / tive   van / ish

long vowel   short vowel

The zebra is a native of Africa. ▶

45

Background and Vocabulary

Selections You Will Read

- "Mountains"
- "To the Top of the World"

"Mountains" is **expository nonfiction.** Expository nonfiction gives facts and information about a topic. As you read, look for:

- headings that begin sections of related information
- photographs and captions

What is "Mountains" about?

This selection is about how mountains change. Forces deep inside the earth cause mountains to form. Water, wind, and weather cause mountains to wear away.

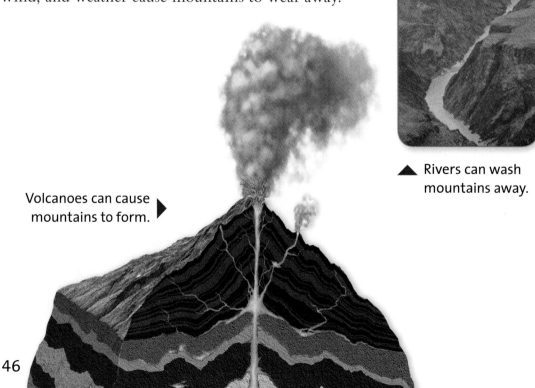

▲ Rivers can wash mountains away.

Volcanoes can cause mountains to form. ▶

What vocabulary will you learn?

Robust Vocabulary

- eruption
- depths
- gradually
- revealed
- contract
- constant
- immediate

Tip

As you learn new words, remember to write them in your Vocabulary Log. Which words do know very well? Which words are you still learning?

Word Bank

climate

temperature

coast

erosion

continents

Comprehension

What is the focus skill in this lesson?

The focus skill is **Text Structure: Cause and Effect.**
Authors of nonfiction texts may organize information in a
cause-and-effect text structure. In texts with this structure,
the author tells what happened (the effect) and why it happened
(the cause). Sometimes a cause has more than one effect.

Read the passage.

> When wind from the Pacific Ocean reaches a mountain, the wind
> slows down. The air rises up. As the air rises, it cools. The moisture
> in the cooling air causes clouds to form. Rain falls from the clouds,
> making the west side of the mountain green.

- **Cause:** A mountain causes air to rise.
- **Effects:** Cooler air, clouds, and rain are some effects of this.

Moist air blown from Pacific Ocean

Dry air moving toward desert

48

Grammar and Writing

What kind of writing will you do in this lesson?

You will write an **informational paragraph.** You will organize your writing by topic sentence and details. Here is a short informational paragraph:

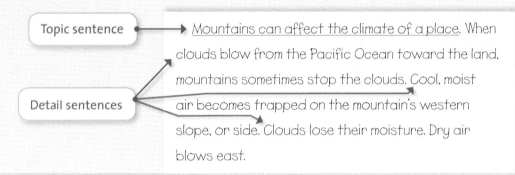

Topic sentence → <u>Mountains can affect the climate of a place</u>. When clouds blow from the Pacific Ocean toward the land, mountains sometimes stop the clouds. Cool, moist air becomes trapped on the mountain's western slope, or side. Clouds lose their moisture. Dry air blows east.

Detail sentences

What is the grammar skill?

You will learn about **singular and plural nouns.**

one wolf ▶   two wolves ▶

Decoding–Spelling Connection

Some words have a **prefix** added at the beginning. A prefix adds meaning.

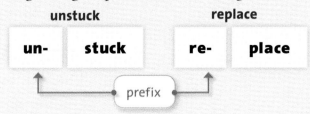

unstuck

| un- | stuck |

replace

| re- | place |

prefix

Background and Vocabulary

Selections You Will Read

- "Fire Storm"
- "Flame Busters"

"Fire Storm" is realistic fiction. Realistic fiction has characters and events that are like people and events in real life. As you read, look for:

- realistic characters and events
- a main character who faces a challenge

What is "Fire Storm" about?

This selection is about a family who gets trapped by a forest fire while they are on a camping trip. Fire cannot burn the same place twice. How do you think this will help the family in "Fire Storm" survive?

What vocabulary will you learn?

Robust Vocabulary

treacherous

drudgery

plunge

smoldering

altered

scoffed

skeptically

discouraged

Tip

Be a Word Detective! Look for these words in newspapers, magazines, and books. Listen for these words on the radio or television.

Word Bank

waterfall

kayaks

paddle

campground

cascade

forest

51

Comprehension

What is the focus skill in this lesson?

The focus skill is **drawing conclusions.** An author does not always explain everything in a story. Sometimes you must put together story details with what you know to understand what you are reading. This is called drawing conclusions.

Read the passage.

> Max came to the clearing in the forest. He saw pieces of blackened wood. He smelled smoke. He saw that smoke was still rising from some pieces of wood.

- The author does not tell you what happened to the forest.
- You can draw the conclusion that a fire has burned part of it.

Grammar and Writing

What kind of writing will you do in the lesson?

You will write a letter. This is an example of a short letter:

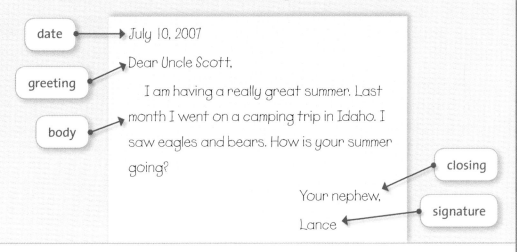

date → July 10, 2007

greeting → Dear Uncle Scott,

body → I am having a really great summer. Last month I went on a camping trip in Idaho. I saw eagles and bears. How is your summer going?

Your nephew,

Lance

closing

signature

What is the grammar skill?

You will learn about **possessive nouns.**

singular possessive noun (belongs to one)	plural possessive noun (belongs to more than one)
the **boy's** kayak	the **boys'** kayaks

Decoding–Spelling Connection

You will learn about suffixes, word parts that are added at the end of words.

-able   *-ible*   *-ness*   *-ment*   *-less*

inflatable

inflate **+** **-able**

53

Background and Vocabulary

Selections You Will Read

- "The Stranger"
- "A Place in the Sun"

THE STRANGER

"The Stranger" is **fantasy.** A fantasy is an imaginative story that may have unrealistic characters and events. As you read, look for:

- story events that could not happen in real life
- characters that may behave in an unrealistic way

What is "The Stranger" about?

The story is about a family who lives on a farm. Late in the summer, they meet a stranger. The stranger stays with them on their farm. Here are some questions the family has about the stranger.

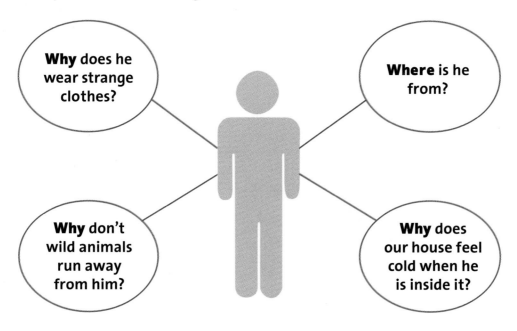

Why does he wear strange clothes?

Where is he from?

Why don't wild animals run away from him?

Why does our house feel cold when he is inside it?

What vocabulary will you learn?

Robust Vocabulary

hermit

fascinated

occasionally

timid

peculiar

drab

trembling

dashed

Tip

Remember to look in the Glossary for explanations of the words. What other strategies can you use?

farmer

Word Bank

autumn

steam

frost

summer

Comprehension

What is the focus skill in this lesson?

The focus skill is **drawing conclusions.** Remember that authors do not always tell readers everything that happens in a story. Sometimes you must use story details and what you know to draw conclusions about what is happening in the text. When you draw conclusions, you figure out something an author has not directly explained.

Read the passage.

> The air was cold, but the sun was shining. Farmer Markley picked many baskets of ripe red apples. He loaded the baskets in his truck and took them to the fruit market. Then he went back to his orchard and picked some more.

- **Story Detail:** A farmer is picking apples
- **What You Know:** Apples get ripe in the fall.
- **Conclusion:** It must be autumn.

Grammar and Writing

What kind of writing will you do in the lesson?

You will write a **pourquoi tale**. *Pourquoi* means "why" in French. A pourquoi tale tells why something happened, or how something came to be. Here is a short pourquoi tale.

Jack Frost is a fantasy character.

Jack Frost has long white hair. A cold wind follows him everywhere he goes. When Jack Frost sits in the branches of a tree, the tree freezes. When he touches a piece of glass, the glass becomes covered with frost. Jack Frost visits the earth every year, at the end of autumn. He brings the winter with him.

The story of Jack Frost explains why winter comes.

What is the grammar skill?

You will learn about **pronouns** and **antecedents**.

<u>The farmer</u> planted <u>corn</u> in the spring. <u>He</u> harvested <u>it</u> in the fall.

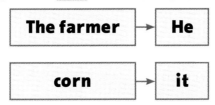

The farmer	→	He
corn	→	it

Decoding–Spelling Connection

The ending /ən/ can be spelled *en, an, ain,* and *on*.

chick **en** but t**on**

cer t**ain**

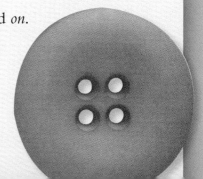

Background and Vocabulary

Selections You Will Read

You will read a selection titled "The Adventurers." The selection is a **Readers' Theater.**

READERS' THEATER

You will also read a selection titled "Icebergs: Floating Snow Cones." This selection is **expository nonfiction.** Remember that expository nonfiction gives facts and information about a topic.

COMPREHENSION STRATEGIES

What are the selections about?

"The Adventurers" is about some fourth graders who spend one week on a sailing ship in the Florida Keys.

"Icebergs: Floating Snow Cones" is about huge chunks of ice that float in the ocean.

the Florida Keys

an iceberg

What vocabulary will you learn?

Robust Vocabulary

hoist

pristine

intrepid

undoubtedly

delectable

seasoned

guidance

privilege

cherish

fragile

Tip

Remember to look in the Glossary for explanations of the words. What other strategies can you use?

Word Bank

sculptures

coral reef

bow

helm

sailing vessel

stern

islands

snorkel and mask

Fluency

As you read "The Adventurers," you will review the two fluency skills you practiced in Theme 3. When you read a script aloud, remember to:

- pay attention to punctuation marks to guide your **pace**
- read with **expression**

Comprehension Strategies

As you read "Icebergs: Floating Snow Cones," you will review the two comprehension strategies you learned in Theme 3.

- **Use Graphic Organizers** Use graphic organizers to help you organize information as you read. Here is one kind of graphic organizer:

| Cause | → | Effect |

- **Read Ahead** If you have questions about what you are reading, read ahead to find the answers.

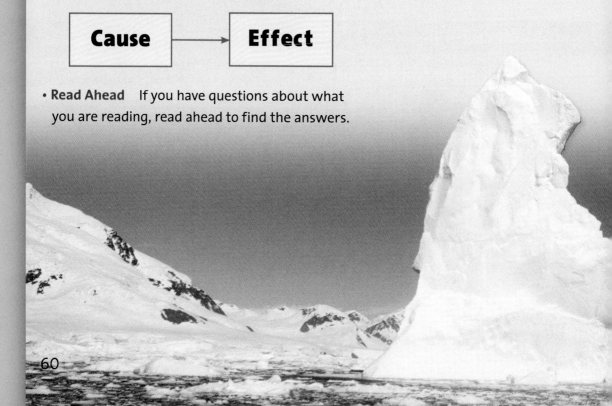

Writing

In Theme 3, you wrote several compositions. In Lesson 15, you will choose one of these compositions to revise. Choose a composition that you would like to add to your Writing Portfolio.

> **Tip**
>
> **Writing Traits** **Conventions** include spelling, punctuation, and capitalization.
>
> When you revise **sentences,** make sure that:
> • you have used different kinds of sentences
> • you have used a mix of long and short sentences

SAMPLE REVISION

Look at how the first paragraph below was revised. What makes the revised paragraph better?

Icebergs form near Greenland. Icebergs form near antarctica. When an iceberg forms, it flotes in the ocean. An iceberg can be green or blue. Or white. Some icebergs are huge. One iceberg is 180 miles long.

Icebergs form near Greenland and Antarctica. After an iceberg forms, it floats in the ocean. Icebergs can be green, blue, or white. Some icebergs are huge! One of the largest is 180 miles long!

Background and Vocabulary

Selections You Will Read

- "So You Want to Be an Inventor?"
- "Make a Movie Machine"

"So You Want to Be an Inventor?" is **narrative nonfiction.** Narrative Nonfiction tells about people, things, events, or places that are real. As you read, look for:

- factual information that tells a story
- illustrations or photographs of real people and places

What is "So You Want to Be an Inventor?" about?

This selection is about inventors—people who create new things to make life easier. These photos show two inventions Thomas Edison helped to develop.

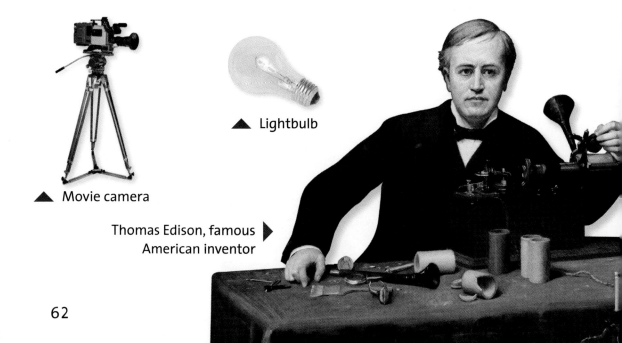

▲ Lightbulb

▲ Movie camera

Thomas Edison, famous American inventor ▶

What vocabulary will you learn?

Robust Vocabulary

tinker

hoaxer

trampled

forged

perfect

quest

barriers

Tip

As you learn new words, remember to write them in your Vocabulary Log. Which words do you know very well? Which words are you still learning?

Word Bank

steamboat

telegraph

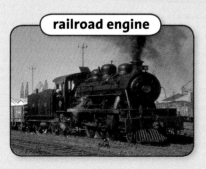
railroad engine

rocket

printing press

Comprehension

What is the focus skill in this lesson?

The focus skill is **Fact and Opinion.** A fact is a statement that can be proved. An opinion is a statement of feeling or belief that cannot be proved. Authors of nonfiction texts may use both facts and opinions in their writing.

Read the passage.

> Thomas Edison was an American inventor. He invented many things, including the light bulb. The light bulb was his most important invention. It changed the way people worked and played.

- The first, second, and fourth sentences are facts.
- The third sentence is an opinion.

Thomas Edison in his laboratory ▶

Grammar and Writing

What kind of writing will you do in the lesson?

You will write a **how-to composition.** In it, you will explain how to do something. Here is a short how-to composition.

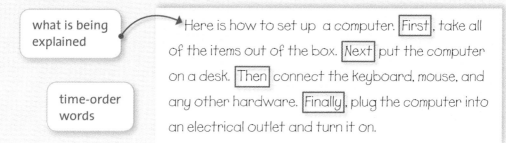

what is being explained

time-order words

Here is how to set up a computer. First, take all of the items out of the box. Next put the computer on a desk. Then connect the keyboard, mouse, and any other hardware. Finally, plug the computer into an electrical outlet and turn it on.

What is the grammar skill?

You will learn about **possessive and reflexive pronouns.**

possessive pronoun

This invention is **mine.**

reflexive pronoun

I built it **myself.**

Decoding–Spelling Connection

The /ər/ ending can be spelled *ar, er,* or *or.* The /əl/ ending can be spelled *al, el, il,* or *le.*

bot**tle**

inven**tor**

Background and Vocabulary

Selections You Will Read

- "Just Like Me"
- "I Am an Artist"

"Just Like Me" is an **autobiography.** An autobiography is a person's account of his or her own life. As you read, look for:

- the first-person point of view
- the author's personal thoughts and feelings
- facts and opinions about the author's life

What is "Just Like Me" about?

In this selection, several artists tell about themselves and their art. Each artist's story includes a photograph of the artist and a self-portrait the artist created.

▼ An artist and her self-portrait

What vocabulary will you learn?

Robust Vocabulary

ancestors

brilliant

exotic

graceful

mischievous

participate

Tip

Be a Word Detective! Look for these words in newspapers, magazines, and books. Listen for the words on the radio or television.

Word Bank

portrait

quilt

sketching

museum

Comprehension

What is the focus skill in this lesson?

The focus skill is **Fact and Opinion.** A fact is a statement that can be proved. An opinion is a statement that expresses a feeling or belief. When people write about their experiences, they usually include both facts and opinions.

Read the paragraph.

> I think Diego Rivera is one of the world's most important artists. He was born in Mexico in 1886. During his career, Rivera created many murals and paintings. His best painting shows a sunset over the ocean.

- **The first and last sentences are opinions.**
- **The second and third sentences are facts.**

Grammar and Writing

What kind of writing will you do in the lesson?

You will write an **autobiographical composition.** In an autobiographical composition, the author tells about events in his or her life. Here is an example of a short autobiographical composition:

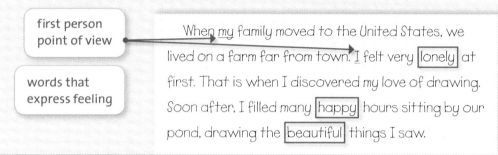

first person point of view

words that express feeling

When my family moved to the United States, we lived on a farm far from town. I felt very lonely at first. That is when I discovered my love of drawing. Soon after, I filled many happy hours sitting by our pond, drawing the beautiful things I saw.

What is the grammar skill?

You will learn about **subject and object pronouns.**

Subject pronoun

Object pronoun

She likes to paint.

I will buy brushes for her.

Decoding–Spelling Connection

The /ər/ ending can be spelled *ar, er,* or *or.*
The /ən/ ending can be spelled *on, en,* or *ain.*

mount**ain**

doct**or**

Lesson 18

Background and Vocabulary

Selections You Will Read

- "Hewitt Anderson's Great Big Life"
- "The Little Fly and the Great Moose"

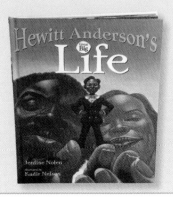

"Hewitt Anderson's Great Big Life" is a **fairy tale.** A fairy tale is an imaginative story that may be retold in different forms. As you read, look for:

- characters with traits that may not appear in real life
- a happy ending

What is "Hewitt Anderson's Great Big Life" about?

This story is about a family of giants. The mother is a giant. The father is a giant. However, their son Hewitt is very, very small.

◄ A *giant* is a very big person.

70

What vocabulary will you learn?

Robust Vocabulary

bountiful

vast

stature

relentless

roused

resourceful

intentions

inadvertently

Tip

Remember to look in the Glossary for explanations of the words. What other strategies can you use?

Word Bank

residence

measuring cup

broom

duet

maze

Comprehension

What is the focus skill in this lesson?

The focus skill is **Theme.** The theme of a story is the message the author wants to share with readers. Authors use setting, characters, and plot to reveal the theme.

- A story's theme is not usually directly stated.
- To determine the theme, look at how characters behave and what they learn.

Read the passage.

Long ago, a sad giant lived in a castle high on a hill. People were afraid of the giant, so no one visited him. One day the giant helped a lost little girl find her way home. She told everyone how kind the giant was.

- The theme is, "Do not judge a person by appearance."

Grammar and Writing

What kind of writing will you do in this lesson?

You will write a **persuasive composition.** You will present an opinion and give reasons why readers should agree with you. Here is a short persuasive composition:

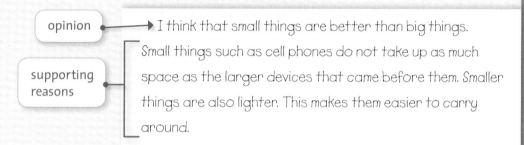

opinion → I think that small things are better than big things.

supporting reasons — Small things such as cell phones do not take up as much space as the larger devices that came before them. Smaller things are also lighter. This makes them easier to carry around.

What is the grammar skill?

You will learn about **adjectives** and **articles.**

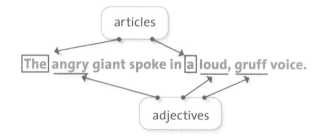

articles

The angry giant spoke in a loud, gruff voice.

adjectives

Decoding–Spelling Connection

The word part *over-* can mean "above." The word part *under-* can mean "beneath." The word part *sub-* can mean "under."

overpass

underwater

submarine

Background and Vocabulary

Selections You Will Read
- "Juan Verdades: The Man Who Couldn't Tell a Lie"
- "Hard Cheese"

"Juan Verdades: The Man Who Couldn't Tell a Lie" is a **folktale.** Folktales are stories that were first told orally. They show the customs and beliefs of a culture. As you read, look for:
- a plot that teaches a lesson
- a main character who shows the values of a culture

What is "Juan Verdades: The Man Who Couldn't Tell a Lie" about?

This folktale is about an honest man who works on a ranch. It tells what happens when the man's honesty is tested.

An **honest** person tells the truth.

A **ranch** is a large farm where cows, sheep, or horses are raised.

What vocabulary will you learn?

Robust Vocabulary

magnificent

insisted

declared

confidently

distressed

gloated

anxiously

Tip

As you learn new words, remember to write them in your Vocabulary Log. Which words do you know very well? Which words are you still learning?

tortillas

Word Bank

apple tree

basket

stump

congratulate

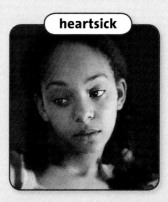
heartsick

Comprehension

What is the focus skill in this lesson?

The focus skill is **Theme.** Remember that the theme is the lesson the author wants readers to understand. To figure out a story's theme, think about what the main character does or learns.

Read the paragraph.

Mario broke his grandmother's favorite plate. He was very worried that she would be upset. Mario thought about saying that the dog had knocked the plate off the table. "No," he thought. "Lying is wrong." So Mario told Grandmother exactly what had happened. She was sad that the plate had broken, but she told Mario she was proud of him for being honest.

The theme is, "Telling the truth is wise."

Grammar and Writing

What kind of writing will you do in the lesson?

You will write a **fable.** A fable is a story that teaches a lesson.
This is an example of a is a fable:

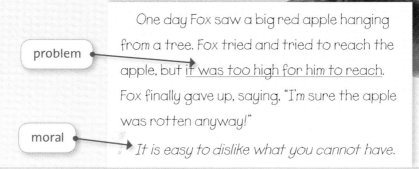

problem

One day Fox saw a big red apple hanging
from a tree. Fox tried and tried to reach the
apple, but it was too high for him to reach.
Fox finally gave up, saying, "I'm sure the apple
was rotten anyway!"

moral

It is easy to dislike what you cannot have.

What is the grammar skill?

You will learn about **comparing with adjectives.**

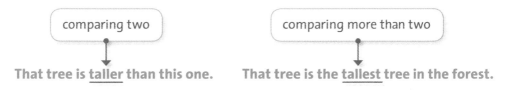

comparing two

comparing more than two

That tree is <u>taller</u> than this one.   That tree is the <u>tallest</u> tree in the forest.

Decoding–Spelling Connection

The endings -*s* and -*es* are added to some words when they
tell about more than one person, place or thing. Other words
change form to tell about more than one.

class ⟷ classes   **tree ⟷ trees**   **mouse ⟷ mice**

An apostrophe (') or apostrophe and s ('s) are added to words
to show possession.

baby ⟷ baby's rattle   **babies ⟷ babies' strollers**

Background and Vocabulary

Selections You Will Read

You will read a selection titled "The Case of the Too-Hot Apple Cider." The selection is a **Readers' Theater.**

You will also read a selection titled "Sequoyah's Talking Leaves." This selection is a **biography.** A biography is the true story of a person's life, written by another person.

READERS' THEATER

COMPREHENSION STRATEGIES

What are the selections about?

"The Case of the Too-Hot Apple Cider" is about two young friends who try to solve a science mystery.

"Sequoyah's Talking Leaves" is about a man who created an alphabet so his people could read and write.

▲ Sequoyah and his alphabet

What vocabulary will you learn?

Robust Vocabulary

ominous

confound

miserable

gracious

beams

self-assurance

monitor

exposed

installed

looming

Tip

As you learn new words, remember to write them in your Vocabulary Log. Which words do you know very well? Which words are you still learning?

Word Bank

lightning

equal amounts

surface area

79

Fluency

As you read "The Case of the Too-Hot Apple Cider," you will review the two fluency skills you practiced in Theme 4. When you read a script aloud, remember to:

- use a **pace** that fits the action in the story
- read words in groups that go together so your **phrasing** is smooth and natural

Comprehension Strategies

As you read "Sequoyah's Talking Leaves," you will review the two comprehension strategies you learned in Theme 4.

- **Monitor Comprehension: Adjust Reading Rate** Adjust your reading rate when you read. When you come to difficult sections of text, read them more slowly.
- **Monitor Comprehension: Self-Correct** As you read, stop to correct any mistakes that make the meaning of the text unclear.

Writing

In Theme 4, you wrote several compositions. In Lesson 20, you will choose one of these compositions to revise. Choose a composition that you would like to add to your Writing Portfolio.

> **Tip**
>
> **Writing Traits** When you revise your writing, try to let your own personal **voice** come through.
>
> Make sure that all your **ideas** are focused on your topic.

SAMPLE REVISION

Look at how the first paragraph below was revised. What makes the revised paragraph better?

> I was born in the city of Memphis, Tennessee. I have two big brothers and one little sister. I hope I am as tall as my brothers someday. We live with our parents and two pets.

> I was born in the bustling city of Memphis, Tennessee. I have two teenage brothers and a freckle-faced little sister. We live with our parents, our parrot, and our big orange cat.

Background and Vocabulary

Selections You Will Read

- "Because of Winn-Dixie"
- "Decoding Dog Speak"

"Because of Winn-Dixie" is **realistic fiction.** A realistic fiction story has characters and events that are like people and events in real life. As you read, look for:

- a setting that could be a real place
- realistic characters and events

What is "Because of Winn-Dixie" about?

This story is about a girl named Opal and her dog, Winn-Dixie. The story tells what happens when Opal and Winn-Dixie go to the library.

▶ A girl with her dog

▲ A library

What vocabulary will you learn?

Robust Vocabulary

consisted

intends

prideful

recalls

select

snatched

Tip

Remember to look in the Glossary for explanations of the words. What other strategies can you use?

hind legs

Word Bank

mosquito

librarian

books

bear

83

Comprehension

What is the focus skill in this lesson?

The focus skill is **Character, Setting, and Plot.** Every story contains one or more characters, a setting, and a plot.

- The **characters** are the people or animals in a story.
- The **setting** is when and where the story takes place.
- The **plot** is the series of events that happen in the story.

Read the paragraph.

characters

setting

plot events

After hiking for an hour, Jack and Tanya stopped to rest. They sat on a large rock under a tall pine tree. A cold wind started to blow. Tanya noticed dark clouds forming in the west. They could see snow on the highest peaks. Tanya looked at the map. Rushing River Pass was still two miles away.

Grammar and Writing

What kind of writing will you do in the lesson?

You will write a **narrative paragraph.** A narrative tells a story. Here is the beginning of a narrative paragraph:

On Saturday afternoon, Jayson went to Lake Park with his dog Farley. When they arrived at the park, Farley rolled happily in the grass. Jayson flopped down next to him. Suddenly a big squirrel darted across the grass. Farley jumped up, barked, and raced after the squirrel at top speed.

What is the grammar skill?

You will learn about **main verbs** and **helping verbs.**

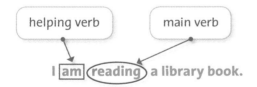

Decoding–Spelling Connection

Suffixes are word parts added to the end of some words. A suffix adds meaning to the word.

Suffix	-ant	-ent	-ist	-ian	-eer
Word	assistant	confident	cyclist	musician	engineer

Background and Vocabulary

Selections You Will Read

- "My Diary from Here to There"
- "Where in the World Did We Come From?"

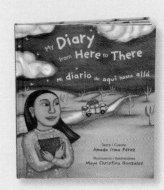

"My Diary from Here to There" is a series of **diary** entries. A diary is a personal account of the author's day-to-day experiences. As you read, look for:

- the first-person point of view
- the author's thoughts about people, places, and events

What is "My Diary from Here to There" about?

This story is about a girl whose family moves from Juárez, Mexico to Los Angeles, California. Their journey is difficult and takes a long time. The family stops in many places along the way.

What vocabulary will you learn?

Robust Vocabulary

burst

opportunities

huddle

comforted

recognizes

journey

Tip

As you learn new words, remember to write them in your Vocabulary Log. Which words do you know very well? Which words are you still learning?

Word Bank

popcorn

braids

escalator

farmworkers

Comprehension

 What is the focus skill in this lesson?

The focus skill is **Character, Setting, and Plot.** Remember that stories contain three main elements: **character, setting, and plot.** The characters and setting work together to shape the plot. Each event in a story affects the events that follow it. Most plots include several events that reveal a conflict or problem that the characters must solve.

Read the passage.

> Henry sat on the steps of his apartment building. A big pile of boxes surrounded him. It was a beautiful, sunny day, but Henry felt sad. The moving truck was parked next to the sidewalk. Henry's friend Raina sat on the steps next to him. "I wish you didn't have to move!" Raina said. "Los Angeles is so far away."

Characters: Henry, Raina

Setting: Henry's apartment building

Plot: Henry must move to a new city. Henry and his friend Raina are sad.

Grammar and Writing

What kind of writing will you do in the lesson?

You will write a **diary entry.** A diary entry tells about your own experiences. This is an example of a diary entry:

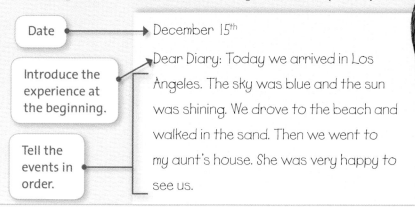

Date	December 15th
Introduce the experience at the beginning.	Dear Diary: Today we arrived in Los Angeles. The sky was blue and the sun was shining. We drove to the beach and walked in the sand. Then we went to my aunt's house. She was very happy to see us.
Tell the events in order.	

What is the grammar skill?

You will learn about **action verbs** and **linking verbs.**

linking verb → We are a family.   action verb → We drove for many miles.

Decoding–Spelling Connection

The word parts *in, out, down,* and *up* appear at the beginning of some words.

in	+	clude	=	include
down	+	stairs	=	downstairs
out	+	cast	=	outcast
up	+	hill	=	uphill

Background and Vocabulary

Selections You Will Read
- "The Cricket in Times Square"
- "Cricket Thermometer"

"The Cricket in Times Square" is **fantasy**. A fantasy is an imaginative story that may have characters and events that are not realistic. As you read, look for:

- characters who behave in an unrealistic way
- story events that happen in time order

What is "The Cricket in Times Square" about?

This selection is about a cat, a mouse, and a cricket who live in a New York City subway station. The subway station is below Times Square.

▲ A subway is a train that goes under the ground.

▲ Times Square is a central area in New York City.

What vocabulary will you learn?

Robust Vocabulary

forlornly

fidget

pathetic

resolved

scrounging

noble

stingy

suspicion

Tip

Be a Word Detective! Look for these words in newspapers, magazines, and books. Listen for the words on the radio or television.

Word Bank

knitting

cash register

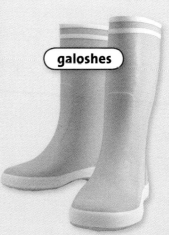

galoshes

janitor

Comprehension

What is the focus skill in this lesson?

The focus skill is **Sequence: Story Events. Sequence** is the order in which events happen. Authors of fiction stories usually write **story events** in sequence. Time-order words such as *first, next, then,* and *finally* help show sequence.

Read the passage.

Our train arrived in New York at 12:01 pm. My brother and I were so excited! We had never been in New York City before. There were so many things we wanted to do. <u>First</u> we went to Central Park. <u>Next</u> we walked to the Metropolitan Museum of Art. Inside the museum there was an entire Egyptian temple! <u>After</u> visiting the museum, we ate hot dogs that we bought from a street vendor. <u>Then</u> we took a taxi back to the train station. <u>Finally</u> it was time to head home.

time-order words

Grammar and Writing

What kind of writing will you do in the lesson?

You will write an **adventure scene.** An adventure scene describes an exciting experience. It uses vivid words to help readers imagine what is happening. Here is the beginning of an adventure scene:

> The elevator doors opened, and Max stepped inside. He was on his way to visit his grandmother, who lived on the eighth floor. Max pushed the shiny button marked "8." The doors shut and the elevator started moving upwards. It stopped on the fourth floor. The door opened, but no one was there. Then a cat strolled into the elevator. A small mouse was riding on its back!

What is the grammar skill?

You will learn about **present-tense verbs.**

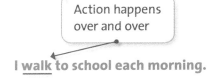

Action happens over and over

I <u>walk</u> to school each morning.

Action happens now

I <u>miss</u> my friend.

Decoding–Spelling Connection

Some words end with one of these suffixes:
-tion, -ation, -ition, -sion, -ial, -al.

ten̲s̲i̲o̲n̲   **fac̲i̲a̲l̲**   **admir̲a̲l̲**   **limit̲a̲t̲i̲o̲n̲**

add̲i̲t̲i̲o̲n̲

Background and Vocabulary

Selections You Will Read

- "Mangrove Wilderness"
- "Mangrove" (an encyclopedia entry)

"Mangrove Wilderness is **expository nonfiction.** Expository nonfiction gives facts and information about a topic. As you read, look for:

- facts and details about a subject or topic
- text structure—the way ideas and information are organized

What is "Mangrove Wilderness" about?

This selection is about a type of tree called the red mangrove. Red mangroves grow in the shallow water along Florida's coastline. Many different plants and animals live in the mangrove wilderness.

▲ Florida

▲ Mangrove trees

What vocabulary will you learn?

Robust Vocabulary

remarkable

suitable

advantage

extract

withstand

stealthy

Tip

Remember to look in the Glossary for explanations of the words. What other strategies can you use?

Word Bank

seedling

food chain

heron

alligator

95

Comprehension

What is the focus skill in this lesson?

The focus skill is **Text Structure: Sequence.** Sequence is one type of text structure, or a way to organize ideas. Authors writing about historical topics use sequence to explain events in history. Authors writing about scientific topics use sequence to describe growth or change in nature.

Read the passage.

The life cycle of a red mangrove includes several stages. First a mature tree blossoms with flowers. About a month later, the flowers fall off the tree. The flowers leave behind fruits. Each fruit contains one seed. When conditions are right, the seeds begin to sprout and grow. After they grow large enough, the young mangrove seedlings fall off the parent tree. These seedlings can float in water until they find a good place to grow. Finally, they take root.

- **Sequence Words:** first, finally

- **Sequence Phrases:** about a month later; when conditions are right; after they grow large enough; until they find a good place to grow

Grammar and Writing

What kind of writing will you do in the lesson?

You will write a **descriptive paragraph** of a setting, or a place. Your paragraph should use details to help readers imagine the place. This is an example of a descriptive paragraph:

> The swamp was full of shadows from the twisted trees. Dark reddish-brown water filled the spaces between the lush plant life. The warm and steamy air smelled of wet earth. Small birds flew past our canoe as we paddled through the trees. The buzz of insects was everywhere.

What is the grammar skill?

You will learn about **past-tense verbs** and **future-tense verbs.**

Past tense

Future tense

I <u>walked</u> to school yesterday.

I <u>will walk</u> to school tomorrow.

Decoding–Spelling Connection

Some words contain more than one suffix.

additional

| add | ition | al |

childishness

| child | ish | ness |

effortlessly

| effort | less | ly |

usefully

| use | ful | ly |

97

Background and Vocabulary

Selections You Will Read

You will read a selection titled "Welcome to Chinatown." The selection is a **Readers' Theater.**

READERS' THEATER

You will also read a selection titled "Amelia's Garden." This selection is **realistic fiction.** Remember that realistic fiction has characters, settings, and events that are like people, places, and events in real life.

COMPREHENSION STRATEGIES

What are the selections about?

"Welcome to Chinatown" is about some TV news reporters who visit a Chinese neighborhood in San Francisco, California.

"Amelia's Garden" is about a girl who plants a flower garden in the middle of a city.

What vocabulary will you learn?

Robust Vocabulary

- destinations
- aspects
- vigorously
- reconstruct
- gorgeous
- festive
- ornate
- symbolize
- expectantly
- misfortune

Tip

Be a Word Detective! Look for these words in newspapers, magazines, and books. Listen for the words on radio or television.

Word Bank

bilingual sign

grocery store

dim sum

lion dancer

Fluency

As you read "Welcome to Chinatown," you will review the two fluency skills you practiced in Theme 5. When you read a script aloud, remember to:

- match your **intonation** to the character's mood
- make sure your **reading rate** is fast enough to hold readers' attention

Comprehension Strategies

As you read "Amelia's Garden," you will review the two comprehension strategies you learned in Theme 5.

- **Use Story Structure**   Use story structure to understand how the characters, setting, and plot events fit together in a story.
- **Ask Questions**   As you read, stop to ask yourself questions about the characters, the setting, or the plot events.

Writing

In Theme 5, you wrote several compositions. In Lesson 25, you will choose one of these compositions to revise. Choose a composition that you would like to add to your Writing Portfolio.

Tip

Writing Traits Look at your **choice of words** and make sure that:
• you have chosen colorful words
• you have used the exact words you need
Conventions include spelling, punctuation, and capitalization.

SAMPLE REVISION

Look at how the first paragraph below was revised. What makes the revised paragraph better?

Last year I wint to a chinese new year parade in San francisco. The lion dancers wore pretty costumes. The air was filled with the sound of firecrackers and the smell of food

Last February I went to a Chinese New Year parade in San Francisco. The lion dancers wore colorful red and gold costumes. The air was filled with the sound of popping firecrackers and the delicious smells of dim sum.

Background and Vocabulary

Selections You Will Read
- "Dragons and Dinosaurs"
- "Saturday Night at the Dinosaur Stomp"

"Dragons and Dinosaurs" is a **magazine article.**
A magazine article gives information on a topic
in an interesting way. As you read, look for:
- information divided into sections with headings
- photographs and illustrations with captions

What is "Dragons and Dinosaurs" about?
This selection is about scientists who study dinosaurs.
The scientists use fossils to help them figure out what
dinosaurs may have been like.

▼ Scientists use what they know to
imagine how dinosaurs looked.

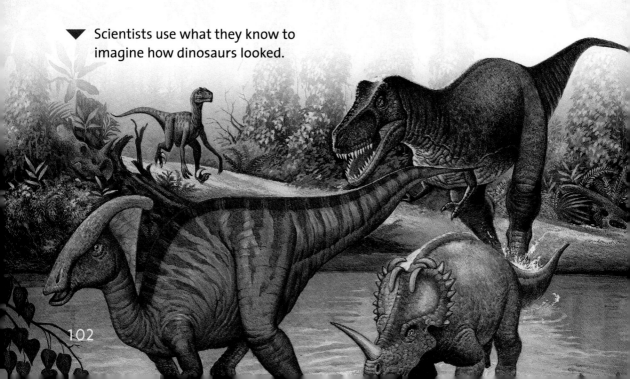

What vocabulary will you learn?

Robust Vocabulary

contraption

roamed

massive

submerged

elegant

obstacles

complicated

eerie

Tip

Be a Word Detective! Look for these words in newspapers, magazines, and books. Listen for the words on the radio or television.

dragon

Word Bank

crest

skull

lizard

museum

skeleton

Comprehension

What is the focus skill in this lesson?

The focus skill is **Main Idea and Details.** The **main idea** is the most important idea in a nonfiction text. Authors often state the main idea in a sentence at or near the beginning of a passage. **Details** are pieces of information that tell more about the main idea.

Read the passage.

> Triceratops was a large plant-eating dinosaur. It lived in North America long ago. The name *Triceratops* means "three-horned face." Fossilized bones from Triceratops were first found in the late 1880s. From these and other fossils, scientists have figured out that Triceratops was about 30 feet long. Scientists think that Triceratops weighed about 12,000 pounds.

- The first sentence gives the **main idea:** Triceratops was a large plant-eating dinosaur.

- The other sentences are **details:** The details tell what Triceratops was like.

Grammar and Writing

What kind of writing will you do in the lesson?
You will write a **summary.** A summary tells the most important information in a passage. Read the passage below. Then read the summary.

> **Passage:** Scientists who study dinosaurs are called paleontologists. These scientists need to know about many different subjects. They study the Earth's history to understand how fossils were created. They study bones to understand what fossils show. They also learn how to use computers to put together the information they find.
>
> **Summary:** Paleontologists must learn about many different things, including Earth's history, fossils, bones, and computers.

What is the grammar skill?
You will learn about **irregular verbs.**

The party **begins** now.

The party **began** an hour ago.

The party **has begun.**

Decoding–Spelling Connection
Some words contain silent letters. Silent letters make no sound when the words are pronounced.

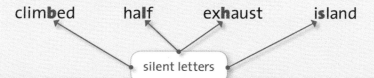

climbed   half   exhaust   island

silent letters

Background and Vocabulary

Selections You Will Read
- "Grand Canyon: A Trail Through Time"
- "The Rock Cycle"

"Grand Canyon: A Trail Through Time" is
narrative nonfiction. Narrative nonfiction tells
about people, things, events, or places that are real.
As you read, look for:
- factual information that tells a story
- paragraphs organized by main idea and details

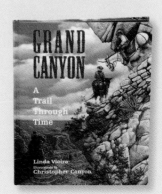

What is "Grand Canyon: A Trail Through Time" about?

This selection is about the Grand Canyon, a long,
deep canyon in the southwestern United States. The
Colorado River runs along the floor of the Grand
Canyon. The Grand Canyon is home to many animals
and plants.

Colorado River ▶

Grand Canyon
▼

What vocabulary will you learn?

Robust Vocabulary

ancient

distant

sentries

glistens

embedded

cascading

weary

eroding

Tip

Remember to look in the Glossary for explanations of the words. What other strategies can you use?

bighorn sheep

Word Bank

mule

gorge

coyote

plateau

Comprehension

What is the focus skill in this lesson?

The focus skill is **Main Idea and Details.** The main idea of a passage is what it is mostly about. Details support, or tell about, the main idea. Sometimes the main idea is not clearly stated in one sentence. Readers use details as clues to figure out the main idea.

Read the passage.

> After breakfast, everyone gathered around the map. The hikers had to figure out which trail to take next. They <u>chose a trail</u> that led to a mountain lake. Then they <u>packed up their food and cooking gear.</u> After that, they <u>took down their tents.</u> When everything was well packed in their backpacks, they <u>walked to the stream</u> and <u>filled their water bottles.</u> Finally they were ready to start hiking.

details {

- The author has not stated the main idea in one sentence.
- You can use the details as clues to figure out that this is the main idea:

  Getting ready for a day of hiking takes a lot of work.

Grammar and Writing

What kind of writing will you do in the lesson?

You will write an **explanatory essay.** An explanatory essay explains something from real life. Here is the beginning of an explanatory essay:

> <u>There are many ways to see the Grand Canyon.</u>
> Most people visit the canyon's south rim. They stand at the top of the canyon and look down into it. Some visitors hike or ride a mule down into the canyon. Other people view the canyon while riding a raft down the Colorado River.

Subject is clearly stated.

What is the grammar skill?

You will learn about **contractions** and **possessive pronouns.**

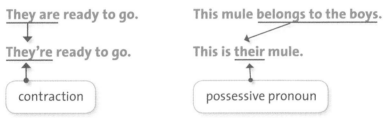

<u>They are</u> ready to go.

<u>They're</u> ready to go.

contraction

This mule <u>belongs to the boys</u>.

This is <u>their</u> mule.

possessive pronoun

Decoding–Spelling Connection

Many words contain Latin or Greek roots.

structure   in**spect**

in**struct**   **spect**ator

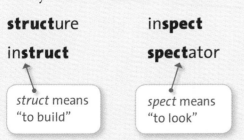

struct means "to build"

spect means "to look"

Background and Vocabulary

Selections You Will Read
- "The Bunyans"
- "Mammoth Cave National Park"

"The Bunyans" is a **tall tale.** A tall tale is a humorous story about impossible events. As you read, look for:
- events that could not happen in real life
- American folk heroes and legends

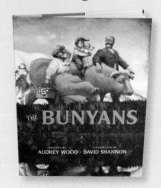

What is "The Bunyans" about?

This story is about a giant named Paul Bunyan and his family. The family travels across the United States, creating famous landforms along the way.

Paul Bunyan is a famous American ▶
tall tale character.

What vocabulary will you learn?

Robust Vocabulary

behemoth

cordially

hearty

fanciful

scenic

colossal

illusion

Tip

As you learn new words, remember to write them in your Vocabulary Log. Which words do you know very well? Which words are you still learning?

Word Bank

lumberjack

geyser

puma

sand dunes

pickax

Comprehension

What is the focus skill in this lesson?

The focus skill is **Figurative Language.** An author may use **figurative language** to help readers picture story events. In figurative language, the meaning of a group of words may be different from the words' individual meanings.

Read the passage.

> Teeny had spent months designing her new collection of clothing for giants. She had worked her fingers to the bone. At last, opening day had arrived. She arranged the dresses and shirts in the front window of her shop. They were a beautiful rainbow of color! Then Teeny looked outside. A line of giants stretched down the street like a huge caterpillar. Teeny was so proud! Her smile was a mile wide as she opened the door.

Idiom: She worked her fingers to the bone.

Metaphor: They were a beautiful rainbow of color!

Simile: A line of giants stretched down the street like a huge caterpillar.

Hyperbole: Her smile was a mile wide.

Grammar and Writing

What kind of writing will you do in the lesson?

You will write a **tall tale.** A tall tale has larger-than-life characters who do things real people cannot do. This is an example of the beginning of a tall tale:

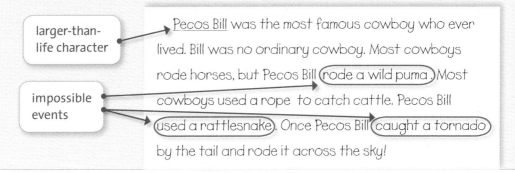

larger-than-life character

impossible events

Pecos Bill was the most famous cowboy who ever lived. Bill was no ordinary cowboy. Most cowboys rode horses, but Pecos Bill rode a wild puma. Most cowboys used a rope to catch cattle. Pecos Bill used a rattlesnake. Once Pecos Bill caught a tornado by the tail and rode it across the sky!

What is the grammar skill?

You will learn about **adverbs.**

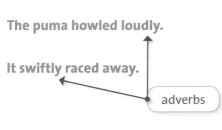

The puma howled loudly.

It swiftly raced away.

adverbs

Decoding–Spelling Connection

Some words sound alike, but are spelled differently and have different meanings.

- Put the book **there.**
- This is **their** project.
- **They're** going to be late.

113

Background and Vocabulary

Selections You Will Read
- "John Muir and Stickeen"
- "John Muir, Extreme Explorer"

"John Muir and Stickeen" is **historical fiction.** Historical fiction is set in the past and portrays people, places, and events that did happen or could have happened. As you read, look for:
- actual historical figures and settings
- historical events told in time order

What is "John Muir and Stickeen" about?

This selection takes place in the Alaska wilderness in 1880. It tells the story of a man named John Muir and a dog named Stickeen.

Alaska

What vocabulary will you learn?

Robust Vocabulary

dedicated

determined

dainty

coddled

pitiful

endured

memorable

avoid

Tip
Remember to look in the Glossary for explanations of the words. What other strategies can you use?

Word Bank

pier

canoe

bow

pinecone

shiver

Comprehension

What is the focus skill in this lesson?

The focus skill is **Figurative Language.** Context clues help readers understand the meaning of figurative language. To understand the meaning of a simile or metaphor, think about the two things the author is comparing.

Read the passage.

> I woke with a start. Panic hit me like a splash of cold water. Mom must have forgotten to wake me up. I looked at the clock—it was 8:00! I was running late! As I began to dress, a hurricane of clothes whirled around my room. Then I happened to look out the window. Snow covered the ground—lots of snow! Mom didn't forget. School must be cancelled because of the snow.

• **Simile:** Panic hit me like a splash of cold water.

• **Idiom:** I was running late!

• **Metaphor:** A hurricane of clothes whirled around my room.

Grammar and Writing

What kind of writing will you do in the lesson?

You will write a **biography.** A biography is a work of nonfiction that tells about a person's life. Here is the beginning of a biography.

> Jedediah Strong Smith was an American trapper and trailblazer. He was born in New York in 1799. As a young man, he worked as a fur trapper. During this time, Smith explored much of the American West. He was among the first people from the United States to travel by land to the area that would become California.

Jedediah Smith State Park, California

What is the grammar skill?

You will learn about **punctuation.** Punctuation includes the use of commas and how to punctuate titles and dialogue.

Commas and Titles	**Tomás, Marta, and Erik enjoyed "John Muir and Stickeen."**
Commas and Dialogue	**"Wow, that story is exciting!" said Tomás.**

Decoding–Spelling Connection

Some words have a prefix, a root, and a suffix.

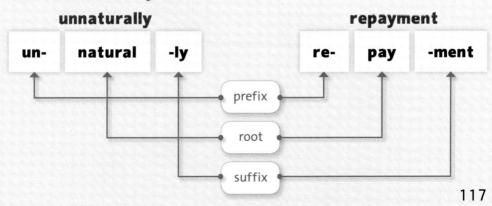

117

Background and Vocabulary

READERS' THEATER

COMPREHENSION STRATEGIES

Selections You Will Read

You will read a selection titled "Discovering the Atocha."
The selection is a **Readers' Theater.**

You will also read a **textbook selection** titled "Producers
and Consumers." "Producers and Consumers" is like a
chapter you might read in a science textbook.

What are the selections about?

"Discovering the Atocha" is about some divers who
find a sunken treasure ship.

"Producers and Consumers" explains how the sun's
energy moves from plants to animals in an ecosystem.

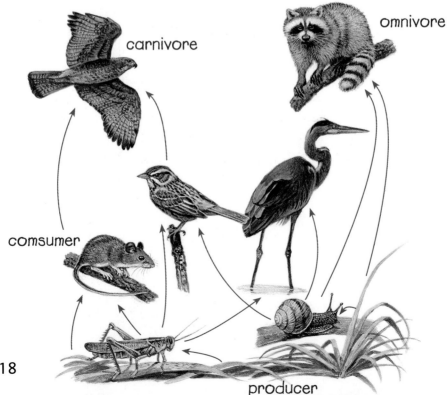

carnivore

omnivore

comsumer

producer

What vocabulary will you learn?

Robust Vocabulary

distinguished

verify

discern

dubious

descend

frantically

estimate

vicinity

abruptly

scrutinize

Tip

Remember to look in the Glossary for explanations of the words. What other strategies can you use?

Word Bank

galleon

cannon

scuba diver

treasure

shipwreck

119

Fluency

As you read "Discovering the Atocha," you will review the two fluency skills you practiced in Theme 6. When you read a script aloud, remember to:

- practice reading each word correctly until you can read your lines with **accuracy**
- read with **expression** that matches your character's personality and emotion

Comprehension Strategies

As you read "Producers and Consumers," you will review the two comprehension strategies you learned in Theme 6.

- **Summarize** As you read, pause to sum up the most important ideas in the text. You can summarize after reading a paragraph, a section of text, or a complete text.
- **Monitor Comprehension: Reread** Monitor comprehension while you read. Reread any sections of text you did not understand.

Writing

In Theme 6, you wrote several compositions. In Lesson 30, you will choose one of these compositions to revise. Choose a composition that you would like to add to your Writing Portfolio.

Tip

Writing Traits

When you revise your writing, make sure that your ideas are **organized** in a way that makes sense.

Make sure that you have used different kinds of sentences to achieve **sentence fluency**.

SAMPLE REVISION

Look at how the first paragraph below was revised. What makes the revised paragraph better?

"Discovering the Atocha" is about a treasure hunter named Mel Fisher. Mel and his crew finally found the Atocha. He and his crew searched for the treasure ship Atocha for 15 years. First they searched the Key of Matecumbe. Mel decided that the Atocha was not there. He learned more about the hurricane that sank the Atocha. He decided that they should search the Marquesas Keys. They searched there for five years.

"Discovering the Atocha" is about a treasure hunter named Mel Fisher. He and his crew searched for the treasure ship Atocha for 15 years. First they searched the Key of Matecumbe, but Mel concluded that the Atocha was not there. After he learned more about the hurricane that sank the Atocha, he decided that they should search the Marquesas Keys. They searched there for five years. Mel and his crew finally found the Atocha!

Using the Glossary

Like a dictionary, this glossary lists words in alphabetical order. To find a word, look it up by its first letter or letters.

To save time, use the **guide words** at the top of each page. These show you the first and last words on the page. Look at the guide words to see if your word falls between them alphabetically.

Here is an example of a glossary entry:

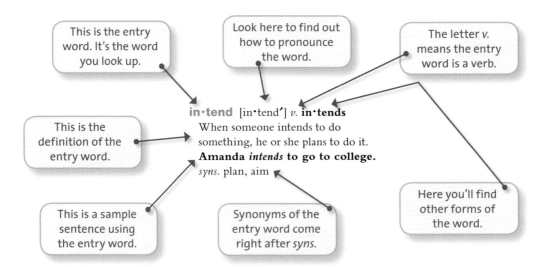

Word Origins

Throughout the glossary, you will find notes about word origins, or how words get started and change. Words often have interesting backgrounds that can help you remember what they mean. Here is an example of a word origin note:

> **Word Origins**
>
> **jostle** *Jostle* comes from the word *joust*, the root of the Old French word *jousten*. It originally came from the Latin word *juxtare*, meaning "to come together." When people bump into each other, they jostle each other.

Pronunciation

The pronunciation in brackets is a respelling that shows how the word is pronounced. The **pronunciation** key explains what the symbols in a respelling mean. A shortened pronunciation key appears on every other page of the glossary.

PRONUNCIATION KEY

a	add, map	m	move, seem	u	up, done
ā	ace, rate	n	nice, tin	û(r)	burn, term
â(r)	care, air	ng	ring, song	yōō	fuse, few
ä	palm, father	o	odd, hot	v	vain, eve
b	bat, rub	ō	open, so	w	win, away
ch	check, catch	ô	order, jaw	y	yet, yearn
d	dog, rod	oi	oil, boy	z	zest, muse
e	end, pet	ou	pout, now	zh	vision, pleasure
ē	equal, tree	ŏŏ	took, full	ə	the schwa, an
f	fit, half	ōō	pool, food		unstressed vowel
g	go, log	p	pit, stop		representing the
h	hope, hate	r	run, poor		sound spelled
i	it, give	s	see, pass		*a* in *above*
ī	ice, write	sh	sure, rush		*e* in *sicken*
j	joy, ledge	t	talk, sit		*i* in *possible*
k	cool, take	th	thin, both		*o* in *melon*
l	look, rule	th	this, bathe		*u* in *circus*

Other symbols:
- · separates words into syllables
- ′ indicates heavier stress on a syllable
- ′ indicates lighter stress on a syllable

Abbreviations: *adj.* **adjective,** *adv.* **adverb,** *conj.* **conjunction,** *interj.* **interjection,** *n.* **noun,** *prep.* **preposition,** *pron.* **pronoun,** *syn.* **synonym,** *v.* **verb**

A

a·brupt·ly [ə·brupt′lē] *adv.* If you do something abruptly, you do it very suddenly. **The baseball game ended *abruptly* when it started to rain.** *syns.* suddenly, unexpectedly

---
Word Origins

abrupt The word *abrupt* comes from the Latin *abruptus,* meaning "broken off or disconnected." The word parts are *ab-* "off" + *ruptus* "break." It originally referred to a rupture or fracture of an arm or a leg. Something that happens abruptly happens in a seemingly broken and disconnected way.

ACADEMIC LANGUAGE

accuracy When you read with *accuracy,* you read without any mistakes.

ac·cus·ing [ə·kyoo′zing] *adj.* When you look at someone in an accusing way, you are showing that you think he or she has done something wrong. **The judge gave Victor an *accusing* look when he thought Victor was guilty.** *syn.* blaming

ad·van·tage [ad·van′tij] *n.* When someone takes advantage of something, he or she makes good use of it. **Nellie and Janine take *advantage* of their neighbor's knowledge of woodworking by asking him for advice on building a birdhouse.** *syns.* benefit, use

al·ter [ôl′tər] *v.* **al·tered** When something has been altered, it has been changed. **Darnel *altered* the look of the old sofa by covering it with new fabric.** *syns.* change, modify

an·ces·tor [an′ses·tər] *n.* **an·ces·tors** The people who came before you in your family are your ancestors. **Alice's *ancestors* came to this country from Poland.** *syn.* forebear

ancestor

an·cient [ān′shənt] *adj.* Something ancient is very, very old. **Scientists in China have discovered the ruins of an *ancient* city that is more than two thousand years old.** *syn.* old

an·noy [ə·noi′] *v.* **an·noyed** To be annoyed means to be somewhat angry about something. **Rachel was *annoyed* when Mary spilled hot chocolate on her homework.** *syn.* irritate

anx·ious·ly [angk′shəs·lē] *adv.* If you waited anxiously for something, you worried about how it would turn out. **As Mr. Donovan handed out the report cards, Leroy waited *anxiously*.** *syns.* nervously, uneasily

as·pect [as′pekt′] *n.* **as·pects** The aspects of a place or thing are its features and elements. **The test has two *aspects*—the reading section and the writing section.** *syns.* feature, part

at·ten·tive [ə·ten′tiv] *adj.* If someone is attentive, that person is carefully listening to or watching something. **The students were *attentive* as they watched the video about the food chain.** *syns.* alert, focused

124

ACADEMIC LANGUAGE

autobiography An *autobiography* is a person's account of his or her own life. Autobiographies use the first-person point of view.

a·vert [ə·vûrt′] *v.* **a·vert·ed** If you averted your eyes, you looked away from something instead of directly at it. **During the eclipse, María *averted* her eyes from the sun.** *syn.* turn away

a·void [ə·void′] *v.* If you avoid a person or thing, you keep away from them. **Chico knows how to *avoid* getting tagged while running from third base to home plate.** *syn.* escape

bar·ri·er [bar′·ē·ər] *n.* **bar·ri·ers** Barriers are objects or people that keep you from moving ahead. **The police put up *barriers* to prevent cars from driving on Main Street during the parade.** *syns.* obstacle, fence

beam [bēm′] *v.* **beams** Someone who beams is grinning. **Denisha *beams* with pride when her hockey team wins the game.** *syn.* smile

be·he·moth [bi·hē′məth] *n.* Something called a behemoth is extremely large. **Scientists describe the prehistoric sloth as a hairy *behemoth*.** *syn.* giant

Word Origins

behemoth *Behemoth* is a Latin word that came from the Hebrew word *b'hemoth,* a plural form of the word *b'hemah,* meaning "beast." The Hebrew word, most likely a version of the Egyptian word *pehemau,* literally means "water-ox," the name for the hippopotamus. The hippopotamus, whose habitat was the Nile River, was the "beast" most feared by the Egyptians, who used the river daily for transportation and trade.

ACADEMIC LANGUAGE

biography A *biography* is the story of a real person's life that is written by another person.

bond [bänd] *n.* A bond is a feeling or interest that unites two or more people or groups. **The twins, Carmen and Isabella, have such a close *bond* that they seem to know each other's thoughts.** *syns.* link, relationship

boun·ti·ful [boun′ti·fəl] *adj.* If you had a bountiful amount of something, you would have a lot of it. **The harvest was so *bountiful* that Maggie's family was eating corn for months.** *syns.* plentiful, abundant

bril·liant [bril′yənt] *adj.* Things that are brilliant are very bright and often shiny. **Emanuel's mom got a necklace with a *brilliant* blue gemstone for her birthday.** *syns.* dazzling, sparkling

a add	e end	o odd	o͞o pool	oi oil	th this	
ā ace	ē equal	ō open	u up	ou pout	zh vision	ə = { a in *above*
â care	i it	ô order	û burn	ng ring	th thin	e in *sicken*
ä palm	ī ice	o͝o took	yo͞o fuse	th thin		i in *possible*
						o in *melon*
						u in *circus*

burst [bûrst] *v.* When a person feels ready to burst if he or she doesn't say something, it means that the person is very excited and cannot wait to say that thing. **Lamont felt that he would** *burst* **if he didn't announce his invitation to attend the International Science Fair.** *syn.* erupt

---

C

cas·cade [kas·kād'] *v.* **cas·cad·ing** Cascading water falls or rushes downward very fast. **A** *cascading* **waterfall flows over Luis's rock garden.** *syn.* flow

cease [sēs'] *v.* If you cease to do something, you stop doing it. **Takara is going to** *cease* **watching television during the week of exams.** *syns.* stop, quit

cher·ish [cher'ish] *v.* If you cherish something, it means a lot to you and you care for it lovingly. **Grandparents** *cherish* **their grandchildren and delight in their visits.** *syns.* treasure, value

FACT FILE

cherish *Cherish* comes from Old French and means "to hold dear." Some state courts have put the word *cherish* into their state constitutions, requiring the government to "cherish education." By this they mean not only to value education but also to support it financially. By law, a state must cherish education by funding it through taxes.

clus·ter [kləs'tər] *n.* **clus·ters** Clusters are small groups of people or things that are close together. **We bought two** *clusters* **of grapes for an afternoon snack.** *syn.* bunch

cluster

cod·dle [kä'dəl] *v.* **cod·dled** Someone who has been coddled has been treated too kindly or protected too much. **Fred's mother** *coddled* **him and wouldn't let him play outside.** *syns.* pamper, overprotect

co·los·sal [kə·lä'səl] *adj.* Something that is colossal is huge. **Many apartment buildings and office buildings in large cities are** *colossal* **skyscrapers.** *syns.* huge, enormous

FACT FILE

colossal The Colossus was one of the Seven Wonders of the Ancient World. This huge statue, which stood at the entrance to the harbor of the Mediterranean island of Rhodes in Greece, was 120 feet high. It was said to be so large that ships could sail between its legs. The word *colossus* comes from the Greek word *kolossos,* meaning "large." Without the statue of the Colossus of Rhodes, the English language would never have included the word *colossal.*

com·fort [kum'fərt] *v.* **com·fort·ed** If a person comforted a friend, he or she helped that friend feel better about something. **When Jane didn't do well on the test, Lisa** *comforted* **her by promising to help her study for the next one.** *syns.* console, reassure

com·mence [kə·mens'] *v.* **com·menced** Something that has commenced has begun. **Zack** *commenced* **doing his homework but was distracted from it when his friend Jacob called.** *syns.* begin, start

com·pli·cated [käm'plə·kā·ted] *adj.* Something that is complicated has many parts that are connected in ways that make it hard to understand. **The engine of a car is a type of** *complicated* **machinery.** *syns.* complex, intricate

com·pre·hend [käm′pri·hend′] *v.* If you comprehend something, you understand it. **Mother couldn't *comprehend* why Natasha didn't like wearing a uniform to school.** *syns.* understand, grasp

---

Word Origins

comprehend The word *comprehend* comes from the Latin verb *comprehendere,* meaning "to grasp or seize." The word parts are *com-,* meaning "completely," and *prehendere,* meaning "to catch hold of or seize." In 1340, the meaning changed to "to grasp with the mind." A person who comprehends something has grasped its meaning.

---

con·fi·dent·ly [kän′fə·dənt·lē] *adv.* When you do something confidently, you are sure about what you are doing. **Sharrita *confidently* entered the spelling bee.** *syns.* self-assuredly, assertively

con·found [kən·found′] *v.* If you confound a person, you surprise or confuse him or her. **Toshi knew she could *confound* her sister by telling her she didn't want to borrow her clothes anymore.** *syns.* confuse, bewilder

con·sist [kən·sist′] *v.* **con·sist·ed** If something consisted of several things, it was made up of those things. **The fruit in the basket *consisted* of bananas, apples, and peaches.** *syns.* comprise, include

con·stant [kän′stənt] *adj.* If something is constant, it happens without stopping. **The *constant* breeze from the ocean is delightful in the summertime.** *syns.* steady, continuous

con·ster·na·tion [kän′stər·nā′shən] *n.* Someone who feels consternation is upset or worried about what is happening. **Bret's *consternation* that the ship might sink did not go away until he was safe on shore.** *syns.* concern, worry

con·tract [kən·trakt′] *v.* To contract means to get smaller by shrinking. **In his report, Pedro explained that heating metal makes it get bigger and that cooling metal makes it *contract*.** *syns.* decrease, shrink

con·tra·dict [kän′trə·dikt′] *v.* **con·tra·dict·ing** Contradicting someone is saying that what the person has said is wrong. **Lupita was *contradicting* Marissa's statements about the advantages of going to a private school.** *syns.* disagree, refute

con·trap·tion [kən·trap′shən] *n.* A contraption is a strange-looking machine or device. **For the science fair, the fourth-grade team built a *contraption* for measuring and pouring chemicals.** *syns.* device, machine

cor·dial·ly [kôr′jəl·ē] *adv.* To say something cordially is to say it in a warm, friendly way. **Elena *cordially* answered the tourists' questions.** *syns.* pleasantly, kindly

crane [krān] *v.* **craned** If you craned your neck, you stretched it to let you see or hear something better. **When the concert started, Akio *craned* his neck to better see the performers.** *syn.* stretch

cringe [krinj] *v.* **cringed** If you cringed, you moved or flinched slightly because of discomfort or fear. **Latisha *cringed* when the dentist started drilling one of her teeth.** *syns.* flinch, wince

a	add	e	end	o	odd	$\overline{oo}$	pool	oi	oil	th	this		
ā	ace	ē	equal	ō	open	u	up	ou	pout	zh	vision		
â	care	i	it	ô	order	û	burn	ng	ring			ə =	*a* in *above*
ä	palm	ī	ice	$\overline{oo}$	took	yōō	fuse	th	thin				*e* in *sicken*

ə = { *a* in *above* / *e* in *sicken* / *i* in *possible* / *o* in *melon* / *u* in *circus*

cu·li·nar·y [kə′lə·ner′ē] *adj.* Culinary skills or tools are related to cooking. **The chef specialized in making desserts that were** *culinary* **masterpieces.** *syn.* cooking

culinary

dain·ty [dān′tē] *adj.* Something that is dainty is small and delicate. **Alberto was afraid of breaking the** *dainty* **china cup.** *syns.* delicate, fancy

---
Word Origins

dainty The word *dainty* is related to the Latin words *dignus,* meaning "worthy," and *dignitas,* meaning "worth or beauty." Old French changed the Latin word to *daintie* and gave it the meanings of "price or value" and "delicacy or pleasure." The adjective was first recorded in 1300, meaning "choice or excellent." Over time, its meaning changed to "delicately pretty." Lace makes a wedding gown look dainty, or delicately pretty.

---

dart [därt] *v.* **dart·ed** An animal that darted moved suddenly and quickly in a particular direction. **The rabbit wandered into the yard, but when it saw the cat, it** *darted* **back into the woods.** *syn.* rush

dash [dash] *v.* **dashed** If someone dashed away, he or she quickly and suddenly ran away. **Matthew** *dashed* **away in a split second when he spotted his younger sister coming out to play.** *syns.* hurry, run

---
FACT FILE

dash The word *dash* came from a Scandinavian source, but it has a varied history of meanings. The oldest sense is found in the phrases *dash to pieces* and *dashed hopes.* Then followed the meanings "to move quickly" and "to write hurriedly." The term *dashboard,* which refers to a part of an automobile, came from an earlier use in 1846 to refer to the board in front of a carriage that stopped mud from being dashed, or splashed, into the vehicle by the horse's hoofs.

---

de·cep·tive [di·sep′tiv] *adj.* A deceptive person or thing tries to make you believe something that is not true. **Brenda's mom realized the advertisement was** *deceptive* **when it stated that the washing machine would work forever.** *syn.* misleading

de·clare [di·klâr′] *v.* **de·clared** Something that has been declared has been announced in a clear way. **Serena's mom** *declared* **that dinner would be ready by 6 o'clock.** *syns.* state, announce

ded·i·cate [de′di·kāt′] *v.* **ded·i·cat·ed** If you are dedicated to achieving a goal, you are devoting yourself to that purpose. **Derrick's teacher is** *dedicated* **to improving the math scores of the class.** *syns.* devote, commit

de·lec·ta·ble [di·lek′tə·bəl] *adj.* A food described as delectable tastes very good. **Lydia baked a *delectable* cake for the party.** *syns.* tasty, delicious

delectable

del·i·cate [de′li·kət] *adj.* If something is done in a delicate way, it is done with great care so that nothing is broken or hurt. **With a *delicate* touch, José removed the new dishes from the carton.** *syn.* fragile

de·prive [di·prīv′] *v.* **de·priv·ing** If someone is depriving you of something, the person is keeping you from having it. **Mom was *depriving* Karl of the last piece of cake until he finished his homework.**

depth [depth′] *n.* **depths** The depths of something are its deepest parts. **Scientists in a minisub found a new species of fish in the *depths* of the ocean.**

de·scend [di·send′] *v.* When you descend, you move downward. **With the elevator broken, Takashi wondered how long it would take to *descend* the fifteen floors by using the stairs.** *syn.* fall

des·ti·na·tion [des′·tə·nā′shən] *n.* **des·ti·na·tions** Destinations are the places people are going to. **The travelers took the shuttle bus from the airport to their *destinations*.**

de·ter·mined [di·tûr′mind] *adj.* A determined person will do everything possible to try to accomplish a task. **Felipe is a *determined* tennis player who practices hitting the tennis ball every day.** *syns.* persistent, resolute

dis·cern [di·sûrn′] *v.* If you discern things, you are aware of them and are able to tell differences between them. **Tia learned to *discern* between a real friend and someone who just wanted to use her things.** *syns.* distinguish, perceive

dis·cour·age [dis·kûr′ij] *v.* **dis·cour·aged** If something discouraged you, it made you believe things weren't going to turn out as you hoped. **Charles was hoping to earn money for a bike, but the lack of after-school jobs *discouraged* him.** *syn.* dishearten

dis·tant [dis′tənt] *adj.* Something distant is very far away. **Sam can't walk to the zoo, because it is too *distant* from his home.** *syns.* far, remote

dis·tin·guished [dis·ting′gwisht] *adj.* A distinguished person stands out from others in a job or field of work. **Carl Sagan, a *distinguished* astronomy professor, was invited to speak at many scientific conventions.** *syns.* famous, prominent

dis·tressed [dis·trest′] *adj.* Someone who is distressed feels very sad and helpless. **Kana was *distressed* to learn that her favorite teacher was leaving.** *syns.* upset, troubled

down·cast [doun′kast′] *adj.* Someone who is downcast is feeling sad and has no hope. **Gabriela was *downcast* when a blizzard ruined her vacation plans.** *syns.* dejected, depressed

a	add	e	end	o	odd	o͞o	pool	oi	oil	th	this		ə =	a in *above*
ā	ace	ē	equal	ō	open	u	up	ou	pout	zh	vision			e in *sicken*
â	care	i	it	ô	order	û	burn	ng	ring					i in *possible*
ä	palm	ī	ice	o͝o	took	yo͞o	fuse	th	thin					o in *melon*
														u in *circus*

drab [drab] *adj.* Something drab looks dull and lacks color. **Awan's living room looks *drab* because all the walls and furniture are in shades of brown.** *syns.* dull, plain

drudg·er·y [drə′jə·rē] *n.* Drudgery is hard and unpleasant or boring work. **Cleaning my room is *drudgery* to me.** *syn.* toil

du·bi·ous [dōō′bē·əs] *adj.* A person who is dubious is doubtful or unsure about something. **Debra's coach was *dubious* about her ability to finish the ten-mile race.** *syns.* doubtful, uncertain

ee·rie [ir′ē] *adj.* Something that is eerie is strange and makes people feel afraid. **The local cemetery at night has an *eerie* atmosphere.** *syns.* creepy, weird

el·e·gant [el′ə·gənt] *adj.* Something elegant is graceful and pleasing to look at. **The design of Molly's dress is *elegant*.** *syn.* stylish

em·bed [im·bed′] *v.* **em·bed·ded** If an object is embedded in something, it is stuck firmly in it. **A splinter was *embedded* in Gusto's finger.** *syns.* stick, entrench

en·cir·cle [in·sûr′kəl] *v.* To encircle a place means to surround it. **Bonnie's plan is to *encircle* the area with traps and wait to see if the ants take the bait.** *syns.* surround, circle

en·dure [in·dŏŏr′] *v.* **en·dured** Someone who has endured hardships has used personal strength to survive them. **Because she had inner strength, Cynthia *endured* the difficult times in her life.** *syns.* survive, outlast

e·rod·ing [i·rō′ding] *adj.* Something that is eroding is being slowly scraped away a little at a time, often by the force of moving water or strong wind. **During the hurricane, the already *eroding* beach lost more sand.** *syns.* weather, wear

e·rup·tion [i·rup′shən] *n.* An eruption happens when something bursts through a surface. **The volcanic *eruption* sent thick clouds of smoke into the sky.** *syn.* explosion

eruption

es·ti·mate [es′tə·māt] *v.* When you estimate an amount of something, you make a careful guess about how many things there are in it. **Tim tried to *estimate* the cost of the bike to make sure he had enough money to buy it.** *syns.* approximate, guess

ex·ist [ig·zist′] *v.* **ex·ists** When something exists, it is a real thing that is present in the world. **Ben found where ants *exist* in his apartment by following their trail to the bread in the cabinet.** *syns.* live, survive

ex·ot·ic [ig·zä′tik] *adj.* Something exotic is unusual and interesting because it came from a faraway place. **Some people consider dates and hummus from the Middle East *exotic* foods.** *syn.* unusual

ex·pec·tant·ly [ik·spek′tənt·lē] *adv.* When you wait expectantly for something, you eagerly look forward to it. **Alisha was *expectantly* awaiting a letter from her grandfather.** *syns.* hopefully, eagerly

ex·pose [ik·spōz′] *v.* **ex·posed** A thing that has been exposed has been uncovered and has lost its protection from its surroundings. **The hurricane blew off the garage roof and *exposed* the car to the wind and rain.** *syn.* uncover

ACADEMIC LANGUAGE

expository nonfiction *Expository nonfiction* text presents and explains facts about a topic. Photographs, captions, and headings are commonly found in these texts.

ACADEMIC LANGUAGE

expression Reading aloud with *expression* means using your voice to match the action of the story and the characters' feelings.

ex·ten·sive [ik·sten′siv] *adj.* Something extensive includes a large amount of things. **Kiyoshi's mother's plans to remodel the kitchen were *extensive* and included new appliances, new cabinets, and new flooring.** *syns.* large, sizable

ex·tract [ik·strakt′] *v.* When you extract something, you carefully pull it out of something else. **The dentist will *extract* two of Stan's teeth.** *syns.* remove, extricate

ex·u·ber·ant [ig·zōō′bər·ənt] *adj.* If someone is exuberant, he or she is full of excitement, energy, and happiness. **Mauricio is *exuberant* about doing a comedy sketch in which he can use lots of facial expressions.** *syns.* enthusiastic, excited

ACADEMIC LANGUAGE

fable A *fable* is a short story that teaches a lesson or moral about life. Fables often include animals as characters.

fairy tale A *fairy tale* is an imaginative story that may be passed down and retold in different forms.

fan·ci·ful [fan′si·fəl] *adj.* Something that is fanciful is not real but comes from the imagination. **In her journal, Lakeisha wrote about her *fanciful* journey to the moon.** *syns.* imaginary, whimsical

fas·ci·nate [fa′sə·nāt′] *v.* **fas·ci·nat·ed** When you are fascinated by something, you are very interested in it and pay close attention to it. **The kitten is *fascinated* by the colorful fish in the aquarium.** *syn.* enthrall

fes·tive [fes′tiv] *adj.* Something that is festive is colorful and exciting. **The holidays are *festive* in Dario's village, as families celebrate with special foods, singing, and dancing.** *syns.* exciting, merry

fidg·et [fi′jət] *v.* People might fidget, or move around restlessly, when they are bored or nervous. **At the movies, Patrice and Frankie annoy everyone when they *fidget* and won't sit still.** *syns.* squirm, move

fierce [firs] *adj.* A fierce person or animal is angry, violent, or ready to attack. **A possum can be *fierce*, attacking with its very sharp teeth.** *syns.* aggressive, violent

flex·i·ble [flek′sə·bəl] *adj.* Something is flexible if it can bend or be bent easily. **Ryan used a *flexible* cord to bundle a stack of newspapers.** *syns.* supple, limber

flinch [flinch′] *v.* **flinched** If a person flinched, he or she quickly moved away from something dangerous or painful. **Aneko *flinched* as the doctor injected the flu vaccine into her arm.** *syns.* recoil, cringe

fluke [flōōk] *n.* A fluke is something unusual that happens by accident. **It was just a *fluke* that Dad found my ring when he was mowing the lawn.** *syn.* coincidence

foist [foist′] *v.* **foist·ed** If something is foisted on you, it is given to you whether you want it or not. **It was not Dan's turn to do the dishes, but the job was *foisted* on him when his brother became sick.** *syns.* impose, force

a	add	e	end	o	odd	ōō	pool	oi	oil	th	this		∂ =	*a* in *above*
ā	ace	ē	equal	ō	open	u	up	ou	pout	zh	vision			*e* in *sicken*
â	care	i	it	ô	order	û	burn	ng	ring					*i* in *possible*
ä	palm	ī	ice	ōō	took	yōō	fuse	th	thin					*o* in *melon*
														u in *circus*

ACADEMIC LANGUAGE

folktale A *folktale* is a story that reflects the customs and beliefs of a culture. Folktales were first told orally and have been passed down through generations in a region or culture.

forge [fôrj] *v.* **forged** If you forged something together, you did it with great effort and you hope it lasts a long time. **Consuela and Daphne *forged* a new work schedule to organize the tasks on the farm.** *syns.* create, build

for·lorn·ly [fôr·lôrn′lē] *adv.* If you do something forlornly, you do it in a way that shows you feel sad and lonely. **After her guests left, Aponi looked around *forlornly* at the empty house.** *syns.* sadly, unhappily

fra·gile [fra′jəl] *adj.* If a thing is fragile, it is easily broken or damaged. **Jenny's mom has special cups that she uses only on special occasions because they are very *fragile*.** *syns.* delicate, frail

fragile

fran·ti·cal·ly [fran′ti·kə·lē] *adv.* To behave frantically is to behave in a wild, energetic way. **When the bus took the turn too fast, Shen and Jason *frantically* grabbed something to hold onto.** *syns.* anxiously, worriedly

ACADEMIC LANGUAGE

functional text *Functional text* is writing used in everyday life, such as letters, manuals, and directions.

fu·ry [fyoor′ē] *n.* Fury is extremely strong anger. **When Jack didn't get his way, he stomped out of the room in a *fury*.** *syns.* anger, wrath

G

gape [gāp] *v.* **gaped** If you gaped at something, you stared open-mouthed in surprise. **As the parade passed by, the crowd *gaped* at the gigantic balloon characters.** *syns.* stare, gawk

glare [glâr] *v.* **glared** If you glared at someone, you stared at the person in an angry way. **Ramon *glared* at Francisco after Francisco laughed at him for slipping in the mud.** *syn.* glower

glis·ten [glis′ən] *v.* **glis·tens** Something that glistens looks wet and shiny. **The lake *glistens* in the sunlight every morning.** *syns.* gleam, sparkle

gloat [glōt] *v.* **gloat·ed** If someone gloated, he or she bragged about something in a mean way. **Showing poor sportsmanship, the winning team *gloated* over its victory.** *syn.* revel

gor·geous [gôr·jəs] *adj.* A gorgeous person or thing is attractive and stunning. **The princess looked *gorgeous* in her gown as she entered the ballroom.** *syns.* beautiful, stunning

FACT FILE

gorgeous *Gorgeous* has roots in the Latin word *gurga*, which became the Old French word *gorge,* meaning "throat." *Gorgeous* was borrowed from the Old French word *gorgias,* meaning "fashionable, elegant, or fond of wearing jewelry." Since a necklace is jewelry worn around the throat, beautiful jewelry came to be described as *gorgeous*.

grace·ful [grās′fəl] *adj.* If a person is graceful, he or she moves in a smooth way that is nice to look at. **A ballet dancer is graceful.** *syns.* elegant, pleasing

gra·cious [grā′shəs] *adj.* Someone who is gracious is pleasant and polite. **Camila was very *gracious* as she welcomed her guests and made them feel at home.** *syns.* courteous, sociable

grad·u·al·ly [gra′jə·wəl·ē] *adj.* Something that happens gradually happens very slowly over time. **Asad is learning his multiplication facts *gradually* by memorizing a different set of facts each week.** *syns.* slowly, progressively

gui·dance [gī′dəns] *n.* Someone who gives guidance provides help and advice. **With her dancing teacher's *guidance,* Annette learned the new tap routine.** *syns.* supervision, direction

---

H

---

heart·y [här′tē] *adj.* If a meal is hearty, it is satisfying and includes plenty of good food. **We always have *hearty* meals at our family reunions.** *syns.* filling, plentiful

her·mit [hər′mət] *n.* A hermit is a person who lives alone, often far from a community. **Far from the city's malls, traffic, and crowds, the *hermit* felt comfortable in his country home.** *syns.* loner, recluse

Word Origins

hermit The word *hermit* has roots in the Greek word *eremos,* meaning "uninhabited." It is also related to the Greek words *eremia,* meaning "desert or solitude," and *eremites,* meaning "person of the desert." Latin changed the Greek *eremites* to *ermita,* and Old French changed *ermita* to *(h)eremit.* The hermit crab is known for its solitary habits, seldom leaving its borrowed shell.

ACADEMIC LANGUAGE

historical fiction *Historical fiction* stories are set in the past and portray people, places, and events that did happen or could have happened.

hoax [hōks] *n.* **hoax·er** Someone who tries to trick people is a hoaxer. **Kelley is a *hoaxer* who pretends to be asleep when she's not.** *syn.* trick

FACT FILE

hoax The phrase *hocus-pocus* is believed to have been invented by magicians to make them sound impressive when performing tricks. Although this phrase is made up of meaningless rhyming words, from *hocus* has come the word *hoax,* meaning "a mischievous trick."

hoist [hoist] *v.* To hoist something is to raise it, often with mechanical help. **Archie and Mike know when to *hoist* the sails and let the wind guide the boat.** *syns.* lift, raise

a	add	e	end	o	odd	ōō	pool	oi	oil	th	this		a in *above*
ā	ace	ē	equal	ō	open	u	up	ou	pout	zh	vision	ə =	e in *sicken*
â	care	i	it	ô	order	û	burn	ng	ring				i in *possible*
ä	palm	ī	ice	ŏŏ	took	yōō	fuse	th	thin				o in *melon*
													u in *circus*

ACADEMIC LANGUAGE

how-to article A *how-to article* gives step-by-step instructions for completing a task or project.

hud·dle [hə′dəl] *v.* When people huddle together, they gather close to each other in a tight group. **The animals *huddled* together in the cold barn to stay warm.** *syns.* cluster, crowd

---

I

---

il·lu·sion [i·loo′zhən] *n.* An illusion is something that is not really what it appears to be. **A pencil in a glass of water looks broken, but this is an optical *illusion*.** *syns.* impression, delusion

illusion

FACT FILE

illusion *Illusion* comes from the Latin *illusionem,* a combination of *il-,* meaning "at" + *ludere,* meaning "to play." Old French changed the meaning to "mocking," or making someone look ridiculous, either playfully or harmfully. *Illusion* entered the English language in 1350 with the meaning "mockery." Then, in 1380, *illusion* changed to mean "misleading appearance." Optical illusions mislead the senses into perceiving what is not real.

im·me·di·ate [i·mē′dē·ət] *adj.* An immediate event is one that happens right away. **Julio knew an *immediate* response was needed to explain how the carpet got so dirty.** *syns.* instant, instantaneous

im·press [im·pres′] *v.* **im·pressed** To be impressed with someone means to admire that person. **Evan was *impressed* when his friend Tanya won first prize at the science fair.** *syn.* awe

in·ad·ver·tent·ly [i′nəd·ver′tent·lē] *adv.* If you do something inadvertently, you do it without meaning to. **The bus stopped so suddenly that Annabelle *inadvertently* stepped on Ricardo's foot.** *syns.* unintentionally, accidentally

in·fest [in·fest′] *v.* **in·fest·ed** If insects or animals infest a place, they are there in large numbers and usually cause damage. **When the large tree fell over, we realized that it had been *infested* by termites.** *syn.* overrun

ACADEMIC LANGUAGE

informational text An *informational text* presents information and facts.

in·sist [in·sist′] *v.* **in·sist·ed** If you insisted on something, you said it very firmly and you refused to change your mind. **Bobby's mother *insisted* that he put on a clean shirt before dinner.**

--- **Word Origins** ---

insist The word *insist* has roots in the Latin word *insistere,* meaning "persist, dwell upon, or stand upon." Its word parts are *in-,* meaning "upon," + *sistere,* meaning "to take a stand." Someone who insists on something takes a stand on it, or feels strongly and firmly about it.

in·spect [in·spekt′] *v.* **in·spect·ing** Someone who is inspecting something is looking at it very carefully. **Dad is *inspecting* the car before we start our vacation.** *syns.* examine, scrutinize

in·spire [in·spīr′] *v.* **in·spires** If something inspires you, it makes you excited about doing something good. **Dustin's social studies teacher *inspires* the class to volunteer in the community.** *syns.* motivate, encourage

in·stall [in·stôl′] *v.* **in·stalled** If you installed a piece of equipment, you put it in to make it ready for use. **Mr. Sims *installed* the new dishwasher at Myra's house.** *syns.* connect, fit

in·tend [in·tend′] *v.* **in·tends** When someone intends to do something, he or she plans to do it. **Amanda *intends* to take her dog for a walk this afternoon.** *syns.* plan, aim

in·ten·tion [in·ten′shən] *n.* **in·ten·tions** Intentions are ideas about what a person means to do. **The teacher has the best *intentions* of helping her students increase their reading rates.** *syn.* purpose

in·ter·ro·ga·tion [in·ter′·ə·gā′shən] *n.* An interrogation is a long period of intense questioning to get information from someone. **The thief was taken to the police station for *interrogation* about other robberies in the neighborhood.** *syns.* questioning, grilling

in·ter·val [in′tər·vəl] *n.* **in·ter·vals** Something that happens at regular intervals is repeated over and over with a certain amount of time in between. **Lanh's schedule at school is divided into six *intervals*, starting with math.** *syns.* gap, period

ACADEMIC LANGUAGE

intonation *Intonation* is the rise and fall of your voice as you read aloud.

in·trep·id [in·tre′pəd] *adj.* A person who is intrepid acts brave because he or she has no fear. **The *intrepid* explorers ventured far from home, not knowing what awaited them.** *syns.* fearless, brave

jos·tle [jä′səl] *v.* **jos·tling** If the people in a crowd push or knock against you, they are jostling you. **The runners were *jostling* for position before the race.** *syns.* push, shove

jostle

Word Origins

jostle *Jostle* comes from *joust*, the root of the Old French word *jousten*. It originally came from the Latin word *juxtare*, meaning "to come together." When people bump into each other, they jostle each other.

jour·ney [jûr′nē] *n.* A journey is a trip from one place to another that usually takes a long time. **Would you like to take a *journey* to the moon some day?** *syns.* trip, voyage

Word Origins

journey *Journey* comes from the Old French word *journée*, meaning "a day's work or travel." Its root word is *jour*, meaning "day." It originated from the Latin word *diurnum*, meaning "a day." The original sense of a journey was a trip that took a day's time.

a	add	e	end	o	odd	o͞o	pool	oi	oil	th	this		*a* in *above*
ā	ace	ē	equal	ō	open	u	up	ou	pout	zh	vision	ə =	*e* in *sicken*
â	care	i	it	ô	order	û	burn	ng	ring				*i* in *possible*
ä	palm	ī	ice	o͝o	took	yo͞o	fuse	th	thin				*o* in *melon*
													u in *circus*

L

FACT FILE

legend In Latin, *legere* means
"to read" and *legenda* were
"things to be read." Centuries ago, *legenda*, or legends,
were narratives about saints or
martyrs and were intended to
glorify people in a religious
way. When fictional elements
were added to the stories, the
meaning of *legends* changed to
"fanciful tales from the past."
Today a person may be called a
"legend in his own time," and a
legendary person may have outstanding accomplishments that
seem "larger than life."

leg·en·dar·y [lej′ənd·âr·ē] *adj.* Someone
who is legendary has a special fame for
something he or she has done. **Eugenie
Clark is *legendary* for swimming with
sharks to study them.** *syns.* famous,
renowned

loom [lo͞om] *v.* **loom·ing** When an event
is looming, it seems likely to happen soon.
**When Paulita got a toothache, she
knew that a visit to the dentist was
looming.** *syn.* threaten

lum·ber [lum′bər] *v.* **lum·bers** When a
person or an animal lumbers, it moves in
a slow and clumsy way. **A large, heavy
animal such as a bear or an elephant
lumbers when it moves.**

lure [lo͞or] *v.* **lures** If something lures you,
it makes you want to go to it, even though
it is dangerous or could get you in trouble.
**Hoshi felt the deep, dark forest *lure* him
to explore its paths.** *syns.* entice, tempt

lurk [lûrk] *v.* **lurked** If something lurked
somewhere, it waited there quietly hidden,
usually before doing something bad. **When
night came, the lion that *lurked* near the
water hole made its attack.** *syn.* skulk

M

ACADEMIC LANGUAGE

magazine article A *magazine
article* gives information on a topic
and usually includes photographs
with captions.

mag·nif·i·cent
[mag·nif′ə·sənt] *adj.*
Something magnificent
is very beautiful and
impressive. **The Eiffel
Tower is *magnificent*
when it is lit up at
night.** *syns.* superb,
splendid

mas·sive [mas′iv] *adj.*
Something massive is
very large and heavy.
**Dinosaurs were
massive creatures.**
syns. enormous, solid

ma·ture [mə·cho͞or′]
adj. A mature person or
animal is fully grown

magnificent

and behaves like an adult. **Dad says my
brother is not *mature* enough to own a
car.** *syns.* adult, grown

mem·o·ra·ble [mem′ər·ə·bəl] *adj.* If
something is memorable, it is worth
remembering or easy to remember. **The
student concert was a *memorable* event
for Fernando's family.** *syn.* unforgettable

mim·ic [mi′mik] *v.* If you mimic a person
or thing, you try to act or look exactly like
that person or thing. **Rochelle and Valerie
tried to *mimic* Juliet's hairstyle.** *syns.*
imitate, copy

mis·chie·vous [mis′chi·vəs] *adj.* Someone
who is mischievous likes to play tricks
on other people. **Sometimes Beth's
mischievous little brother draws pictures
on her homework.** *syn.* impish

mis·er·a·ble [miz′ər·ə·bəl] *adj.* A person who feels miserable feels uncomfortable and unhappy. **When Sue had chicken pox, she was itchy and *miserable*.** *syns.* uncomfortable, unhappy

mis·for·tune [mis·fôr′chən] *n.* Misfortune is something unlucky or unpleasant that happens to someone. **The storm brought *misfortune* when the bridge collapsed and people were stranded.** *syns.* disaster, hardship

mon·i·tor [mon′ə·tər] *v.* When you monitor something, you regularly check its progress. **Uncle Charlie will help us *monitor* the growth of the tomato plants.** *syns.* watch, observe

mut·ter [mut′ər] *v.* **mut·tered** If you muttered, you said something very quietly because you did not want it to be heard. **Jimar *muttered* about her disappointment in her team's loss.** *syns.* murmur, mumble

ACADEMIC LANGUAGE

mystery A *mystery* is a story that centers on answering questions such as *Who did it?*, *Where is it?*, or *What happened?*

ACADEMIC LANGUAGE

narrative nonfiction *Narrative nonfiction* tells about people, things, events, or places that are real.

ACADEMIC LANGUAGE

narrative poem A *Narrative poem* is a poem that tells a story. Narrative poetry often contains figurative language.

nim·ble [nim′bəl] *adj.* If someone is nimble, he or she moves quickly, lightly, and easily. **Acrobats exercise every day to stay *nimble*.** *syns.* quick, lively

no·ble [nō′bəl] *adj.* If you describe someone as noble, you think that person is honest and unselfish. **Thao did a *noble* deed when he shopped for his elderly neighbor after the ice storm.** *syns.* fine, gallant

nur·ture [nûr′chər] *v.* If you nurture a living thing, you care for it while it is growing and developing. **The mother bear will *nurture* her cubs until they can survive on their own.** *syns.* cultivate, nourish

ob·sta·cle [ob′stə·kəl] *n.* **ob·sta·cles** Obstacles are things that get in your way when you are going somewhere or trying to reach a goal. **Delays caused by traffic and a shortage of parking spaces were *obstacles* to getting Inez to her recital on time.** *syns.* impediment, barrier

obstacle

a	add	e	end	o	odd	o͞o	pool	oi	oil	th	this		a in *above*
ā	ace	ē	equal	ō	open	u	up	ou	pout	zh	vision	ə =	e in *sicken*
â	care	i	it	ô	order	û	burn	ng	ring				i in *possible*
ä	palm	ī	ice	o͝o	took	yo͞o	fuse	th	thin				o in *melon*
													u in *circus*

ob·vi·ous [ob′vē·əs] *adj.* If something is obvious, it is so easily seen or understood that no one has to explain it. **When Clayton's mom entered the living room, it was *obvious* that the dog had torn apart the sofa cushions.** *syns.* apparent, evident

oc·ca·sion·al·ly [ə·kā′zhən·əl·ē] *adv.* If something happens occasionally, it happens once in a while. **Raul *occasionally* goes camping with his family.** *syn.* sometimes

om·i·nous [om′ə·nəs] *adj* Something ominous is a sign of trouble or a warning that something bad is going to happen. **At the opening of the play, the audience heard an *ominous* sound just before the scenery came tumbling down.** *syns.* threatening, menacing

op·por·tu·ni·ty [op′·ər·tōō′nə·tē] *n.* **op·por·tu·ni·ties** Opportunities are chances to do something you want to do. **Keith and Polly are looking for *opportunities* to do volunteer work in a hospital.** *syn.* chance

or·nate [ôr·nāt′] *adj.* Something that is ornate is decorated with a lot of complicated patterns. **During ceremonies, some kings and queens wear *ornate* garments and jewels.** *syns.* fancy, elaborate

ornate

ACADEMIC LANGUAGE

pace Reading at an appropriate *pace* means reading with smoothness and consistency, not too quickly or too slowly.

pact [pakt] *n.* A pact is an agreement between people or countries in which they promise to do certain things. **Rob and Leron made a *pact* to be partners on the science project.** *syns.* deal, agreement

par·ti·ci·pate [pär·tis′ə·pāt′] *v.* If you participate in a game, you are involved in it. **To become a well-rounded athlete, William will *participate* in a different sport each season.** *syns.* partake, join

par·tic·u·lar [pər·tik′yə·lər] *adj.* Something that is particular is one specific thing of its kind. **A boxer is a *particular* breed of dog.** *syn.* specific

pa·thet·ic [pə·thet′ik] *adj.* A person or thing that is pathetic is sad or helpless. You usually feel sorry for pathetic people or things. **The drenched kitten looked *pathetic*.** *syns.* pitiable, sad

pe·cul·iar [pi·kyōōl′yər] *adj.* Something that is peculiar is strange and unusual, usually not in a good way. **The basketball coach was breathing in a very *peculiar* way, so Florence called for help.** *syns.* odd, strange

pen·sive [pen′siv] *adj.* Someone who is pensive is thinking deeply about something. **After reading the book, Nikko was *pensive*, reliving the events in his mind.** *syn.* thoughtful

Word Origins

pensive The word *pensive* has roots in the Latin word *pensare,* meaning "to weigh or to consider." It also is related to the Latin word *pendere,* meaning "to hang or weigh." In jewelry, *pendants* are like little weights that hang down from a necklace. Old French changed *pensare* to *penser,* with the meaning "to think," from which came the adjective *pensif.* English borrowed this word, and it became *pensive.* A pensive person is "weighed down" in thought.

per·fect [pər·fekt′] *v.* To perfect something is to improve it so that it is the best it can be. **Lucy had to *perfect* her piano solo before the concert.** *syn.* polish

ACADEMIC LANGUAGE

phrasing *Phrasing* is grouping words into meaningful "chunks," or phrases, when you read aloud.

pit·i·ful [pit′i·fəl] *adj.* If something is pitiful, it is so sad and weak that people feel sorry for it. **The dog acted *pitiful* so people would feed it.** *syns.* sad, pathetic

ACADEMIC LANGUAGE

play A *play* is a story that is meant to be performed for an audience. Plays often include stage directions that tell the characters how to act. Plays may be broken up into acts and scenes.

pli·a·ble [pli′ə·bəl] *adj.* Something that is pliable is easy to move or bend without breaking. **Jeff made a bowl out of the clay while it was still *pliable.*** *syn.* flexible

plunge [plunj] *v.* If you plunge into something, you rush into it suddenly. **Enrique *plunged* into the water to find his sister's bracelet.** *syn.* dive

ACADEMIC LANGUAGE

poetry *Poetry* is a form of expressive writing in verse.

pounce [pouns] *v.* **pounced** A person or animal that pounced on something jumped on it eagerly to take it. **When Mario dropped the toy mouse, the cat *pounced* on it.** *syns.* swoop, jump

ACADEMIC LANGUAGE

pourquoi tale A *pourquoi tale* is an imaginative story that tells how or why something came to be. Pourquoi tales usually describe how things came to be in nature.

pred·a·tor [pred′ə·tər] *n.* **pred·a·tors** Predators are animals that kill and eat other animals. **Zebras live together in herds to protect themselves from *predators* such as lions.** *syn.* attacker

predator

a add	e end	o odd	o͞o pool	oi oil	th this
ā ace	ē equal	ō open	u up	ou pout	zh vision
â care	i it	ô order	û burn	ng ring	
ä palm	ī ice	o͝o took	yo͞o fuse	th thin	

ə = { a in *above* / e in *sicken* / i in *possible* / o in *melon* / u in *circus* }

pre·serve [pri·zûrv′] *v.* To preserve something is to keep it from being harmed or changed. **The government helps** *preserve* **the natural areas by making laws to protect the wildlife in them.** *syns.* protect, maintain

pride·ful [prīd′fəl] *adj.* A person is prideful if he or she feels very satisfied because of something he or she has done. **Justin felt** *prideful* **after winning first-prize at the science fair.** *syns.* vain, haughty

pris·tine [pris′tēn′] *adj.* If a place is pristine, it is clean and untouched. **Iliana's family was happy to be moving from the crowded city to the** *pristine* **countryside.** *syns.* pure, unspoiled

priv·i·lege [priv′ə·lij] *n.* A privilege is a special advantage or right that only certain people can have. **Hinto and Tehya had earned the** *privilege* **of extra computer time.** *syns.* advantage, benefit

---

Q

quea·sy [kwē′zē] *adj.* If you feel queasy, you have a sick feeling in your stomach. **When the teacher announced a pop quiz, Earl felt** *queasy.* *syns.* sick, nauseous

quest [kwest] *n.* A quest is a journey with a specific purpose. **The knight began his** *quest* **to find the missing princess.** *syn.* mission

---

R

ACADEMIC LANGUAGE

reading rate Your *reading rate* is how quickly you can read a text correctly and still understand what you are reading.

realistic fiction *Realistic fiction* stories have characters, settings, and plot events that are like people, places, and events in real life. The characters face problems that could really happen.

re·call [ri·kôl′] *v.* **re·calls** When a person recalls something, he or she remembers it. **Armando** *recalls* **the fun he had on his eighth birthday.** *syns.* remember, recollect

rec·og·nize [re′kig·nīz] *v.* **rec·og·niz·es** If someone recognizes you, it means they know who you are when they see you. **Nori's teacher** *recognizes* **him in the mall and says hello.** *syn.* know, identify

re·con·struct [rē′kən·strukt′] *v.* To reconstruct something that has been damaged or destroyed means to rebuild it. **The earthquake survivors have begun to** *reconstruct* **their damaged homes.** *syns.* restore, repair

re·cruit [ri·krōōt′] *v.* When you recruit someone, you get him or her to join a group for a special purpose. **Dad had to** *recruit* **Rashan and Tyrone to help him put together the new cabinet.** *syn.* enlist

re·lent·less [ri·lent′ləs] *adj.* Someone who is relentless in trying to do something keeps at it and refuses to give up. **The climber was** *relentless* **in his attempt to reach the mountaintop.** *syns.* persistent, unyielding

re·luc·tant [ri·luk′tənt] *adj.* If someone is reluctant to do something, he or she does not want to do it. **Denise was** *reluctant* **to tell her parents about her low math score.** *syn.* hesitant

re·mark·a·ble [ri·mär′kə·bəl] *adj.* A remarkable thing is something very special in a way that makes other people notice it. **Charlene's** *remarkable* **drawings of her favorite cartoon characters won first place in the art contest.** *syns.* extraordinary, outstanding

rem·i·nis·cent [rem′ə·nis′ənt] *adj.* If something is reminiscent of something else, it brings back memories of that other time or place. **Grandfather said that the Thanksgiving feast was** *reminiscent* **of holiday meals long ago.** *syns.* evocative, suggestive

re·sem·ble [ri·zem′bəl] v. **re·sem·bles** If one person or thing resembles another, the two look similar. **Everyone says that my sister resembles me.**

resemble

re·solve [ri·zolv′] v. **re·solved** When you have resolved to do something, you have made up your mind to do it. **John resolved to learn to drive by his sixteenth birthday.** *syns.* decide, vow

FACT FILE

resolve The word *resolve* is from the Latin word *resolvere,* meaning "to loosen or undo." It is related to the word *solve,* whose meaning "explain or answer" came about in 1533 and became related to the word *solution.* The term's mathematical use was recognized in 1737. A problem can be answered by "undoing" it part by part until it is solved.

re·sound [ri·zound′] v. **re·sound·ed** It a place resounded with a sound, it became filled with that sound. **The empty house resounded with laughter after the family moved in.** *syns.* echo, reverberate

re·source·ful [ri·sôrs′fəl] adj. A resourceful person is good at finding ways to solve problems. **Without enough money for real flowers, the resourceful decorator made paper roses.** *syns.* ingenious, inventive

re·spon·si·ble [ri·spon′sə·bəl] adj. If someone is responsible, that person can be trusted to do a job on his or her own. **Lian would be allowed to get a dog only if he agreed to be responsible for taking care of it.** *syns.* accountable, answerable

re·veal [ri·vēl′] v. **re·vealed** When something is revealed, it was hidden but can now be seen. **As Roger got closer to the huge sculpture, the lines connecting the pieces were revealed.** *syns.* disclose, divulge

━━━ **Word Origins** ━━━

reveal The word *reveal* has origins in the Latin word *revelare,* meaning "to uncover or disclose." *Revelare* literally means "to unveil," from *re-,* which can mean "opposite of," and *velare,* meaning "to veil or cover." Old French changed *revelare* to *reveler,* which English borrowed. To uncover something is to reveal it.

roam [rōm] v. **roamed** If a creature roamed an area, it wandered around there. **At one time, herds of buffalo roamed the Great Plains.** *syns.* wander, travel

rouse [rouz] v. **roused** If you roused someone, you woke up or alerted that person. **The alarm clock roused Ginny so she wouldn't be late for school.** *syns.* awaken, stir

rum·ple [rum′pəl] adj. **rum·pled** Something is rumpled if it is wrinkled or messy. **Kareem fell asleep on the long ride, and when he woke up, his shirt was rumpled.** *syn.* wrinkle

a add	e end	o odd	o͞o pool	oi oil	th this	
ā ace	ē equal	ō open	u up	ou pout	zh vision	ə = { a in above, e in sicken, i in possible, o in melon, u in circus
â care	i it	ô order	û burn	ng ring	th thin	
ä palm	ī ice	o͝o took	yo͞o fuse	th thin		

S

scan [skan] *v.* To scan a place is to look carefully over the entire area for something specific. **Rosalie had to *scan* the crowd in the auditorium to find where her dad was sitting.** *syn.* skim

sce·nic [sē′nik] *adj.* A scenic place has lovely natural features, such as trees, cliffs, or bodies of water. **Juan stopped the car so that he could enjoy the *scenic* ocean view.** *syn.* picturesque

scenic

scoff [skof] *v.* **scoffed** If you scoffed at something, you spoke about it in a mocking or critical way. **Eloise *scoffed* at Hubert's suggestion that they dress up to go to the football game.** *syns.* mock, ridicule

scrounge [skrounj] *v.* **scroung·ing** If an animal is scrounging, it is looking around trying to find food. **The hungry dog was *scrounging* through the garbage cans for food.** *syn.* rummage

scru·ti·nize [skrōō′tə·nīz′] *v.* When you scrutinize something, you examine it carefully to find out some information about it. **Mom thought she saw a tiny bug, so she decided to *scrutinize* the lettuce before using it.** *syns.* examine, inspect

sea·soned [sē′zənd] *adj.* A person who is seasoned at something has a lot of experience with that thing. **After working with the cook in the restaurant for several months, Salma felt she was a *seasoned* chef.** *syns.* experienced, skilled

se·lect [sə·lekt′] *adj.* A select group is one that is special and among the best of its kind. **The owner of the orange grove made up a boxful of *select* oranges for his special guests.** *syns.* best, elite

self-as·sur·ance [self′·ə·shoor′əns] *n.* People who have self-assurance are confident and sure of themselves. **The coach gives the team members a pep talk before the game to give them *self-assurance*.** *syn.* confidence

sen·try [sen′trē] *n.* **sen·tries** Sentries are people who stand as guards around a camp, building, or other area. **The king posted *sentries* around his castle.** *syns.* guard, patrol

se·rene·ly [si·rēn′lē] *adv.* If something is done serenely, it is done in a calm and quiet way. **The day seemed peaceful as Leon sat *serenely* under the tree watching the sunset.** *syns.* calmly, peacefully

siz·zle [siz′əl] *v.* **siz·zles** If something sizzles, it is very hot and makes a hissing sound. **When the bacon *sizzles*, the egg cooks, and the toast is done, it's time for breakfast.** *syns.* crackle, sputter

skep·ti·cal·ly [skep′ti·kə·lē] *adv.* If you speak skeptically about something, you express doubt about whether it is true. **Francine's father listened *skeptically* to her excuses for not doing homework.** *syns.* doubtfully, unbelievingly

slick [slik] *adj.* If something is slick, it is presented in an attractive way. **Eleanora's new black computer monitor looks *slick*.** *syns.* impressive, striking

smol·der [smōl′dər] *v.* **smol·der·ing** Something smoldering is burning slowly from the inside, without flames. **After the fire was out, the cabin was still *smoldering*.** *syn.* burn

snatch [snach] *v.* **snatched** If you snatched something, you grabbed it or pulled it away quickly. **Joan walked into the playroom and *snatched* her teddy bear out of her younger brother's hands.** *syns.* grab, seize

snick·er [snik′ər] *v.* **snick·er·ing**
Snickering is laughing quietly in an unkind way at what someone says or does. **We heard Miguel *snickering* when Rendrick poured juice instead of syrup on his pancakes by mistake.** *syns.* mock, scoff

sol·emn·ly [sol′əm·lē] *adv.* When you say something solemnly, you say it in a very serious way. **Mrs. Pressman spoke *solemnly* as she told the students about their classmate's accident.** *syns.* seriously, somberly

sol·i·tar·y [sol′ə·târ′·ē] *adj.* To live in a solitary way is to be alone most of the time. **The guidance counselor spoke with Harriet about changing her *solitary* way of life.** *syns.* lonely, aloof

---
Word Origins

solitary The word *solitary* originates from the Latin word *solitarius,* meaning "alone or lonely." It has roots in *solitas,* meaning "loneliness," and *solus,* meaning "alone."

---

spar·kle [spär′kəl] *v.* **spar·kling** Something that is sparkling is shining, clear, and bright. **The jewel was so shiny, it was *sparkling*.** *syn.* twinkle

sparkle

stat·ure [stach′ər] *n.* A person's stature is his or her height. **Ramona may be small in *stature,* but she has big ideas.** *syns.* height, size

stealth·y [stel′thē] *adj.* A stealthy animal is one that stays quiet and hidden as it moves about, so that others do not notice it. **The turkeys did not notice the *stealthy* fox hiding behind the rock, lying in wait to make its move.** *syns.* sneaky, furtive

stern [stûrn] *adj.* Someone who is stern is very serious and strict. **Belita's aunt is very *stern* about making visitors take off their shoes before entering her house.** *syn.* strict

stin·gy [stin′jē] *adj.* Someone who is stingy doesn't like to spend money or share what they have. **Karly thinks her brother is *stingy* because he won't give her money when the ice-cream truck comes around.** *syn.* miserly

stroll [strōl] *v.* To stroll is to walk in a slow, relaxed way. **On Sundays, Chim and Felix *stroll* in the park with their families.** *syns.* walk, amble

stun [stun] *v.* **stunned** When someone is stunned by something amazing, he or she is shocked and sometimes even speechless. **The announcement that she had been given the lead part in the play *stunned* Jean.** *syns.* shock, amaze

sub·merge [səb·mûrj′] *adj.* **sub·merged** If something is submerged, it is beneath the surface of a body of water. **The boys couldn't reach the watch because it was *submerged* at the bottom of the pool.** *syn.* immersed

a add	e end	o odd	o͞o pool	oi oil	th this		*a* in *above*
ā ace	ē equal	ō open	u up	ou pout	zh vision		*e* in *sicken*
â care	i it	ô order	û burn	ng ring		ə =	*i* in *possible*
ä palm	ī ice	o͝o took	yo͞o fuse	th thin			*o* in *melon*
							u in *circus*

---- **Word Origins** ----

submerge The word *submerge* comes from the Latin word *submergere,* meaning "to sink or to overwhelm." It is made of two parts: *sub-,* meaning "under," + *mergere,* meaning "to plunge, dip, or immerse." *Submerge* is commonly used in connection with submarines, which travel underwater.

suit·a·ble [so͞oʹtə·bəl] *adj.* Something is suitable if it is right for whatever it is being used. **That purple velvet robe will make a *suitable* costume for the king in the play.** *syn.* appropriate

surge [sûrj] *n.* If you feel a surge of a particular feeling, you feel it suddenly and very strongly. **I felt a *surge* of "spring fever" as I took out the camping gear.** *syn.* gush

sur·ren·der [sə·renʹdər] *v.* When you surrender, you stop fighting something or someone. **Amy and Tamecia refused to *surrender* to the rule that girls are not allowed on the football team.** *syns.* relinquish, concede

---- **Word Origins** ----

surrender The word *surrender* comes from the Old French word *surrendre,* meaning "to give up or deliver over." It is made up of two parts: *sur-,* meaning "over," + *rendre,* meaning "to give back." A considerate young person will surrender his or her seat on a bus to an older person.

sus·pi·cion [sə·spishʹən] *n.* If you think someone is guilty of doing something wrong, you have a suspicion about him or her. **When Brent's lunch money was missing, he had a *suspicion* that his sister had raided his backpack.**

swerve [swûrv] *v.* **swerved** If a car swerved, it turned suddenly to avoid hitting something. **The car *swerved* to avoid hitting the deer that had suddenly jumped across the road.** *syn.* veer

sym·bo·lize [simʹbəl·īzʹ] *v.* If an animal or object symbolizes something, it represents that thing. **On the American flag, the thirteen stripes *symbolize* the original 13 colonies, and the 50 stars stand for the current number of states.** *syn.* represent

symbolize

ACADEMIC LANGUAGE

tall tale A *tall tale* is a humorous story about impossible or exaggerated happenings. Many tall tales are stories about American folk heroes and legends.

taut [tôt] *adj.* Something that is taut has been stretched or pulled very tightly. **When Margaret's mother makes the beds, she pulls the sheets *taut*.** *syns.* tight, firm

ACADEMIC LANGUAGE

textbook *Textbooks* are organized through chapter titles and headings within chapters. They provide information without an author's opinions.

tim·id [timʹid] *adj.* A timid person is shy and unsure of himself or herself. **Wally was so *timid* that he was afraid to enter the room if he was late for class.** *syns.* shy, hesitant

tink·er [tingʹkər] *v.* When you tinker with something, you try to fix or adjust it. **Alita doesn't want Doug to *tinker* with any of the musical instruments.** *syn.* meddle

trait [trāt] *n.* **traits** Traits are particular qualities or characteristics of a person or thing. **Vincente's sister has *traits*, such as being quiet and shy, which are very different from his own loud mannerisms.** *syns.* characteristic, feature

---
Word Origins

trait The word *trait* comes from the Latin word *tractus,* meaning "a drawing." It later came to mean "a drawn line or feature." The sense of the word further extended to mean "a particular feature or distinguishing quality." Middle French borrowed it and made it *trait.* People can be described by their personality traits.

---

tram·ple [tram′pəl] *v.* **tram·pled** If you trampled something, you stepped on it very hard and damaged it. **Nick walked carefully through the flowerbed so that the plants would not get *trampled*.** *syn.* crush

treach·er·ous [trech′ər·əs] *adj.* Something treacherous is dangerous and unpredictable. **Emilio knew it was a *treacherous* situation when he saw the cottonmouth snake in the yard.** *syns.* dangerous, unsafe

---
Word Origins

treachery The word *treachery* comes from the Old French word *trecherie,* meaning "deceit or cheating." It is related to *trique,* meaning "trick." Playing a mean trick on a person is using treachery to mislead him or her.

---

trem·ble [trem′bəl] *v.* **trem·bling** If something is trembling, it is shaking slightly. **Jalissa was *trembling* as she told the park ranger she had seen a bobcat.** *syns.* wobble, shake

un·doubt·ed·ly [un′dou′tid·lē] *adv.* If something will undoubtedly happen, it will definitely happen. **Social studies will *undoubtedly* be Hien's favorite subject this year, as it was last year.** *syns.* unquestionably, doubtlessly

u·nique [yōō·nēk′] *adj.* Something is unique if it is the only one of its kind. **Actresses attending award shows want their gowns to be *unique*.** *syns.* exclusive, distinctive

---
FACT FILE

unique The word *unique* was not commonly used until 1850. From the Latin word *unus,* meaning "one," it became *unicus,* meaning "single." It was then borrowed by the French, who changed it to *unique,* meaning "solitary." Its original meaning in English was "one of a kind," but through extended meanings, things that are unusual, rare, or distinctive are now called unique. For example, an unusual piece of jewelry may be called "unique," even though other similar pieces exist.

---

un·tan·gle [un′tang′gəl] *v.* **un·tan·gled** If you untangled something, you untied knots in it or straightened it if it was twisted. **Eva patiently *untangled* the yarn from the ball that her cat had played with.** *syn.* unravel

---

a	add	e	end	o	odd	ōō	pool	oi	oil	th	this
ā	ace	ē	equal	ō	open	u	up	ou	pout	zh	vision
â	care	i	it	ô	order	û	burn	ng	ring		
ä	palm	ī	ice	ōō	took	yōō	fuse	th	thin		

ə = { a in *above*, e in *sicken*, i in *possible*, o in *melon*, u in *circus* }

V

vast [vast] *adj.* Something that is vast is so wide it would be hard to get across it. **The Grand Canyon is a *vast* North American landmark.** *syns.* huge, enormous

ven·ture [ven′chər] *n.* A new venture is a project that is exciting and even risky. **The brothers were excited about their new business *venture*, selling frozen pizzas.** *syn.* project

Word Origins

venture The word *venture* is a shortened form of *adventure*. *Adventure* comes from the Latin *aventura* and is related to *advenire,* meaning "to come about." Originally, the meaning was "to arrive," but Middle English changed it to "a risky undertaking." It has the general sense of being a daring project.

ver·i·fy [ver′ə·fī′] *v.* If you verify something, you check to make sure that it is true by using very careful research. **Kishawn used an encyclopedia to *verify* information about the largest fish in the world.** *syns.* confirm, prove

vi·cin·i·ty [vi·sin′ə·tē] *n.* If something is in the vicinity, it is nearby. **Yoshi lives in the *vicinity* of the school.** *syns.* neighborhood, locality

Word Origins

vicinity The word *vicinity* comes from the Latin word *vicinitas,* meaning "neighborhood." *Vicinitas* is related to *vicus,* meaning "a group of houses." Neighbors live in a group of houses that make up a neighborhood.

vig·or·ous·ly [vig′ər·əs·lē] *adv.* If you do something vigorously, you do it with energy and enthusiasm. **Bonita *vigorously* mixed the batter so the cake wouldn't be lumpy.** *syns.* forcefully, energetically

viv·id [viv′id] *adj.* Something that is vivid has very bright colors. **Tina chose *vivid* pinks and yellows for her painting of spring flowers.** *syns.* bright, colorful

Word Origins

vivid The word *vivid* is from the Latin word *vividus,* meaning "animated or lively." It is related to the Latin word *vivus,* meaning "alive." The word has come to mean "something strong and clear." This meaning was extended to colors in 1665. In writing, teachers suggest using *vivid* verbs and adjectives to produce strong and colorful mental images.

vul·ner·a·ble [vul′nər·ə·bəl] *adj.* A person or an animal that is vulnerable is weak and unprotected and at risk of being harmed. **Ocean fish are *vulnerable* to shark attacks.** *syns.* defenseless, susceptible

W

wea·ry [wir′ē] *adj.* If you are weary, you are very tired from working hard at something and you want to stop. **The camper was *weary* from hiking all day.** *syns.* tired, exhausted

with·stand [with·stand′] *v.* If you withstand a difficult time, you are able to get through it all right. **Jamie was able to *withstand* his teammates' teasing after he struck out last night.** *syns.* endure, survive

Photo Credits

Placement Key: (t) top, (b) bottom, (l) left, (r) right, (c) center

vi (b) ©DLILLC/Corbis; xi (b) ©Mike King/Corbis; 3 (br) ©Michel Tcherevkoff/The Image Bank/Getty Images; 7 (bc) ©Leo Dennis Productions/Jupiterimages; 7 (cl) ©Tobias Titz/fStop/Getty Images; 8 (b) © Duomo/Corbis; 10 (br) © Jorma Jämsen/zefa/Corbis; 11 (br) © 2006 Jupiterimages Corporation; 11 (cr) © Tim Ridley/Dorling Kindersley/Getty Images; 13 (cr) © Michael DeYoung/Corbis; 15 (bl) ©2006 Jupiterimages Corporation; 15 (bc) ©Anders Ryman/Corbis; 15 (bl) ©Wendell Webber/Jupterimages; 16 (b) ©Bettmann/Corbis; 19 (br) ©2006 Jupiterimages Corporation; 19 (cr) ©Alexandra Grablewski/Jupiterimages; 19 (cl) ©Hispanica/Jupiterimages; 26 (b) ©Royalty-Free/Crobis; 27 (tr) ©Craig Aurness/Corbis; 27 (br) ©Royalty-Free/Corbis; 27 (cl) ©Royalty-free/Corbis; 28 (b) ©Envision/Corbis; 29 (tr) © Craig Aurness/Corbis; 33 (br) © Old Mother Goose from "My Nursery Story Book," pub. by Blackie & Son (book illustration), Adams, Frank (fl. 1903)/, Private Collection/The Bridgeman Art Library; 42 (bc) (c) Ralph A. Clevenger/Corbis; 42 (bl) © D. Robert & Lorri Franz/Corbis; 53 (cl) © Natalie Fobes/Corbis; 58 (cr) © Blueberg/Alamy; 59 (cr) © Arne Pastoor/Jupiterimages; 59 (bc) ©B.S.P.I./Corbis; 63 (cl) © Magnus Rietz/Jupiterimages; 63 (br) © North Wind Picture Archives/Alamy; 64 (br) © Superstock/Jupiterimages; 64 (bl) © Wendell Metzen/Jupiterimages; 68 (b) © Resource, NY ART148544 ; 69 (br) © 2006 Jupiterimages; 71 (bl) © Royalty-free/Corbis; 72 (b) ©Walter Bibikow/The Image Bank/Getty Images; 75 (br) © 2006 Jupiterimages Corporation; 75 (tr) © EVANS CAGLAGE/Dallas Morning News/Corbis; 75 (bl) © Stockbyte Platinum/Alamy; 76 (b) © 2006 Jupiterimages Corporation; 79 (br) © Peter Gridley/Photographer's Choice RF/Getty Images; 83 (bl) © Royalty-free/Corbis; 87 (bc) © 2006 Jupiterimages Corporation; 90 (bl) © Alan Schein Photography/Corbis; 91 (bl) © 2006 Jupiterimages Corporation; 91 (tr) © 2006 Jupiterimages Corporation; 91 (br) ©2006 Jupiterimages Corporation; 91 (c) ©David Toase/Photodisc Green/Getty Images; 94 (br) © William Gray/Jupiterimages; 95 (tr) © 2006 Jupiterimages Corporation; 96 (b) ©Mark Boulton/Alamy; 99 (cr) ©Derek Trask/Corbis; 99 (bl) ©Heath Robbins/Jupiterimages Corporation; 99 (tr) ©Keren Su/Corbis; 103 (tr) ©2006 Jupiterimages Corporation; 103 (tl) ©Highlights for Children/Jupiterimages; 103 (bl) ©Louis Psihoyos/Corbis; 103 (br) ©Pat Canova/Jupiterimages; 104 (b) ©Highlights for Children/Jupiterimages; 107 (bc) ©2006 Jupiterimages Corporation; 108 (b) ©Steve Satushek/Jupiterimages; 109 (br) ©James Lemass/Jupiterimages; 113 (cr) ©James Gritz Photography/Jupiterimages; 115 (br) ©2006 Jupiterimages Corporation; 115 (cr) ©Comstock/Jupiterimages; 116 (b) ©Layne Kennedy/Corbis; 119 (tr) ©Image Source/Alamy; 126 (bl) Artville, Imspace Systems Corporation; 130 (tr) age fotostock/ SuperStock

All other photos from Harcourt School Photo Library and Photographers.

Illustration Credits

Cover Art: Laura and Eric Ovresat, Artlab, Inc.